D1603280

The GLOBETROTTER'S guide to HAPPINESS

The GLOBETROTTER'S guide to HAPPINESS

KATE MORGAN

Illustrated by

JULIET SULEJMANI

Hardie Grant

TRAVEL

CONTENTS

Introduction   vi

Aloha spirit, USA   x

Coffee ceremony, Ethiopia   8

Crystal and stone healing, USA and Canada   16

Dolce far niente, Italy   24

Fika, Sweden   32

Friluftsliv, Norway   42

Gezelligheid, The Netherlands   50

Gross National Happiness (GNH), Bhutan   56

Hygge, Denmark   64

Ikigai, Japan   72

Meraki, Greece   80

Pura vida, Costa Rica   88

Romanticism, England   96

Shinrin yoku, Japan   106

Sisu, Finland   116

Slow Food, Italy   124

Tai chi, China   132

Ubuntu, South Africa   140

Yoga, India   148

Zen meditation, Japan   158

Further reading   168

Index   170

About the author   173

INTRODUCTION

Wherever we are in the world, as humans we're all striving for happiness – a feeling of wellbeing and a sense of calm amidst the everyday life routine and sometimes chaos. What differs around the globe is how we pursue that happiness.

Over recent years, health and wellness has been trending off the charts and this has fuelled a booming industry as people seek an escape from the stress and anxiety of the modern world. Many people are seeking out alternative methods and looking to other countries to learn from other cultures in the pursuit of happiness.

From searching for ikigai (the meaning of life) in Japan, or taking part in the ancient practice of yoga in India, to heading into nature to clear the mind using friluftsliv (free air life) in Norway and appreciating the art of gezelligheid (the feeling of togetherness and cosiness) in The Netherlands, the world is a tapestry of happiness and wellbeing philosophies.

As a travel writer for over a decade now, I've been fortunate enough to have a job where I get to learn about different cultures, experience adventures, discover myriad cuisines, meet a host of interesting people, and be an observer of the lifestyles and customs of people around the globe. From this I've learned a lot – mostly that we can all learn from each other.

I'm extremely thankful for being fortunate enough to make a living from travel writing – it's an amazing job. But at times the glamour fades and it can be a gruelling and challenging one, too. Travel can be a stressful, unhealthy and tiring activity, even if it's for a holiday, and when you add work commitments and deadlines on top of that, the stress and exhaustion is intensified.

I've run what feels like marathons for departing trains and buses with a heavy backpack strapped on, and lugged a suitcase up and down countless flights of stairs to the detriment of my back and knees. I've lost count of how many hours I've tried to get comfortable on rock-hard seats in airports waiting for delayed flights. I've been chased by a moose in Alaska, and had my car break down for hours in the middle of a Zimbabwean national park with plenty of lions, bull elephants and buffalo around but not a scrap of phone reception! I've trekked for hours in Uganda searching for gorillas through forest so dense it's actually named the Impenetrable Forest. I've been hospitalised for a bacterial infection from some dodgy berries I ate in Thailand. I've suffered heat stroke on the Great Wall of China, and caught a load of stomach bugs and other strange illnesses I hope to never have again.

Of course these are also experiences I wouldn't change for the world, as for every challenging travel experience there have been hundreds of incredible ones. After the first couple of years working as a travel writer, I soon realised that if I was going to be able to sustain being on the road for months at a time working, looking after my health and wellbeing needed to become a top priority.

I started trying to find ways to keep myself healthy, both in my body and mind, when I travelled – otherwise

I knew the job could not be sustainable in the long-run. I looked to the destinations I spent time in and how locals approached their health and wellbeing. I regularly travel to Japan and always try to make time to participate in Zen meditation classes at a temple in Kyoto. I also love to head out for time in nature, hiking in the mountain towns of Kurama and Kibune, or the verdant hills of Takao or walking around the Fuji Five Lakes region.

I sought out yoga classes when I visited Mysuru (Mysore) in India, and visited a coffee plantation in Africa where I was honoured to take part in a fascinating and relaxing hours-long coffee ceremony. Whenever I travel to Italy one of my favourite ways to take a break is to order a coffee or aperitivo (pre-dinner drink) in a piazza, put my phone and my notes away and just watch Italian life go by for a while – true dolce far niente (the sweetness of doing nothing). In Amsterdam the iconic brown cafes with their gezellig atmosphere provided me with the perfect spots to rest and reset when researching that city. When I lived in London and was in need of a little beauty and inspiration, I would often visit the Tate Britain to admire the evocative works of Romantic masters Turner and Constable. I learned the meaning of the Greek philosophy of meraki (doing something with devotion and passion), while watching musicians play in the squares of the charming mountain town of Anogia in Crete.

Happiness is an elusive pursuit and everyone's perception of happiness and what it means for them differs. Researching and experiencing the way other countries and cultures define happiness and wellbeing has been a thoroughly fascinating and enlightening experience. When you read through the collection of philosophies in this book, you'll be able to identify the main threads and themes that run through all of them. Notably, wealth and material possessions are absent. What seems to be important to most cultures is cultivating relationships, strong bonds and connections with family, neighbours and friends. Healthy living and a good diet is a key element throughout, as is spending time in nature, living a slower-paced life and avoiding as much stress as possible. Disconnecting from devices, taking time to reflect on what's meaningful to us and enabling our creativity to grow are all part of many of these wellness philosophies.

Each chapter gives ideas on ways you can make these philosophies part of your own daily life – and you don't even need to travel to do it, although I have also given recommendations about where to experience each wellness concept in its country of origin.

To reap the benefits doesn't require significant or fundamental changes – just small ways of changing habits or introducing activities that will hopefully lead you to a healthier, more relaxed and, ultimately, happier you.

Kate Morgan

ALOHA SPIRIT

USA

WHAT IS ALOHA SPIRIT?

Most people are familiar with the term 'aloha'. We've seen movies and concerts where Elvis dons his Hawaiian shirt and plays the ukulele. We've seen hula dancers in grass skirts shaking their hips and tourism ads with 'aloha' splashed across a background resembling paradise. But what does aloha spirit actually mean? How can you truly define something that is so ingrained in Hawaiian society and deeply rooted in its cultural traditions? Something that speaks to the hearts and minds of an island state and acts as a guiding principle for its way of life?

If you have visited Hawaii, you will have heard the word aloha more than a few times over the course of your stay on the Hawaiian Islands. Aloha is used to say hello and goodbye. You might have been greeted at the airport with a lei placed around your neck and a friendly smile and 'aloha' to welcome you to the state. But it's much more than that. It also means love, compassion, goodwill, honour and peace. It's not simply a word in Hawaii but a life force. Hawaiians live and breathe aloha spirit, it's one of the most important values in Hawaiian culture and a defining characteristic of who the people are. Aloha spirit is also about treating other people with care, respect and kindness – looking out for one another.

WHERE DOES THE ALOHA SPIRIT LAW ORIGINATE?

You might've seen the final *Seinfeld* episode where Jerry, Elaine, George and Kramer get arrested under the Good Samaritan Law for not helping out someone being mugged and thought that this law is a bit far-fetched. Well, think again. Aloha spirit is so important to Hawaiians that there is actually a state law for it – the Aloha Spirit Law! According to this law, all citizens, businesses and government officials must conduct themselves with aloha spirit and treat people with the same respect and care as their ancestors did.

The Aloha Spirit Law didn't come into effect until 1986, but Hawaiians have been living their lives by the guiding principle of aloha for as far back as they can recall – it is deeply entrenched in the native culture.

The 1970 Governor's Conference in Hawaii sought to solicit the public's opinion on what they thought the year 2000 in Hawaii should look like. People gathered to discuss the past, present and the future. One of the beloved Maui elders, 'Aunty' Pilahi Paki, delivered a speech in which she spoke about aloha spirit and broke down the word into a phrase for each letter. This became the basis for the Aloha Spirit Law.

A stands for akahai, meaning kindness,
to be expressed with tenderness;

L stands for lōkahi, meaning unity,
to be expressed with harmony;

O stands for ʻoluʻolu, meaning agreeable,
to be expressed with pleasantness;

H stands for haʻahaʻa, meaning humility,
to be expressed with modesty;

A stands for ahonui, meaning patience,
to be expressed with perseverance.

WHAT ARE THE HEALTH AND HAPPINESS BENEFITS?

Many recent studies show that Hawaiians live longer, have lower stress levels and are generally happier than any other state in the USA. Hawaii has continued to have the longest life expectancy rate in the USA, and a 2017 report by the Center for Disease Control and Prevention (CDC) found that despite the overall USA life expectancy rate declining in recent years, Hawaii's is still increasing and the average life expectancy for Hawaiians is 81.3 years.

In 2018, Hawaii topped the Overall Well-being ranking in the USA for the seventh time in a row, according to a survey conducted by Gallup, which started recording the US Well-being Index scores in 2008. The findings were based on more than 115,000 surveys with American adults across all 50 states throughout the entire year of 2018. The five essential metrics used in calculating the Wellbeing Index score were: enjoying your career, having supportive social relationships, being active and in good physical health, feeling safe and having pride in your community, and being free of economic and financial stress. Hawaii was the only state to rank in the top five across all of these metrics.

While we can't say simply that aloha spirit is entirely responsible for these findings, it is plausible that Hawaiians have got something right by living a life that is guided by love and respect for their community and the land – not sweating the small things.

WHERE IN HAWAII CAN I EXPERIENCE ALOHA SPIRIT?

In short – everywhere!

You won't go five minutes in Hawaii before hearing aloha, and it will continue throughout your trip. And you'll soon find you'll be greeting every friendly face you meet there with an 'aloha!' yourself.

As aloha spirit extends far beyond just the word, you'll also see it reflected in Hawaiians' behaviour and actions. You'll feel aloha in the community mindset, in their carefree 'no worries' attitude, and in the way the natural surroundings inspire people's happiness and outlook on life. Aloha spirit isn't something that's only relevant to how we treat other people, it's also about Hawaiians' love and respect for the sacred land.

HOW CAN I MAKE ALOHA SPIRIT PART OF MY DAILY LIFE AT HOME?

Anyone can weave a bit of aloha spirit into their everyday lives and it extends far beyond slipping on a pair of flip-flops, a Hawaiian shirt, tucking into some Spam or hitting the surf. It can be in small ways – to show your community and your local land love, respect and kindness. Here are some ways to help you find your aloha spirit.

GET ACTIVE IN NATURE

Heading out for time in nature is a great way to feel close to aloha spirit. The ocean is a particularly special place, so go for a swim, jump on a surfboard or stand-up paddleboard – whatever takes your fancy. If you can't get to a beach, go for a hike in the countryside, bushland or mountains. If you live in a city, you might simply stroll through a park, or walk along a creek trail or riverside observing the rhythms of the water.

SLOW DOWN AND TAKE YOUR TIME

You might be used to a busy lifestyle where your days whizz past in a flash as you rush around to get everything done. Make a real effort to try to slow things down and show a bit of ahonui (patience). Hawaiians are known for operating on 'island time', where the clock doesn't rule the day so much, and the pace of life is slower. Get outdoors and really focus on what's happening around you, swap social media scrolling for stargazing or escape to the countryside for some R&R. It gives you time to think, to observe the world around you and have time for others, as well as for yourself.

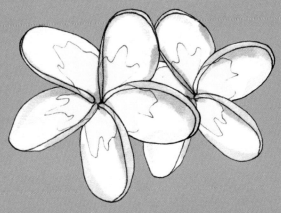

LOOK ON THE BRIGHT SIDE

Staying positive is a key part of aloha spirit. Don't let things get you down; instead try to rise above it. It's not easy to do but if you can, stay in control of your emotions, take deep breaths when something angers you or irritates you, smile and try to look on the bright side. It can do wonders for your mood and helps in controlling your actions.

Why not jot down your feelings in a journal? Just the simple act of letting it out and on to the page can help identify where you're at and help you stay on top of your emotions before they become too overwhelming.

Exercise is another great way of shedding negative emotions and getting those endorphins working for you, so head off with a friend for a long walk.

FOCUS ON RELATIONSHIPS

Having strong family ties and relationships with the people around you is a crucial part of Hawaiian culture and aloha spirit. Treat people with kindness and compassion, and not only your immediate family but also your neighbours, your colleagues, and the people you interact with at the local shops. If you don't know many people, join a bookclub or volunteer at a local charity or not-for-profit. Happiness studies consistently show that people who have strong relationships are more likely to lead happier and more meaningful lives.

COFFEE CEREMONY

ETHIOPIA

WHAT IS THE COFFEE CEREMONY? -.

Ethiopia is the birthplace of coffee, and Ethiopians have been joining together over a hot brew for centuries; to be invited to a coffee ceremony is a sign of respect and friendship. The jebena buna (coffee ceremony), as it's known in the local Amharic language, is a crucial part of Ethiopian society and culture and considered to be the most important social interaction in many towns and villages. Coffee is cherished and the ceremony is a significant time to share with friends and family – just hope you're not in any rush, as the coffee ceremony is a slow-paced, lengthy ritual. No quick take-away in your reusable cup here – the ceremony can last several hours! That's precisely what makes this such a special event – it is highly ritualised and deliberately slow.

The coffee ceremony usually follows a specific format and begins once a meal is over, but it can be at any time of the day. The host is always female and she will start by scattering an assortment of cut grass and flowers on the ground, while the air fills with the aroma of frankincense or perhaps sandalwood wafting from an incense burner. Coffee beans are first washed,

then roasted in a long-handled wok-like pan until black, and guests are invited to move closer to smell the delicious aroma. Next, the hostess will grind the beans with a mortar and pestle and add it to water boiling in a pot called a jeben.

Once the coffee is brewed, the hostess will artfully pour it in a single stream into small ceramic cups for each guest, using a high and skilfully well-aimed pour. Often, the coffee has plenty of sugar added to it and it's considered polite for guests to drink at least three cups from the same grounds of coffee. If you're a latte lover you're mostly likely out of luck as milk is not typically offered. The first cup, called the abol, is the strongest, naturally, the second cup is called tona and the bereka is the third cup. Each cup is said to transform your spirit and the third cup is said to convey a blessing to the drinker. Blessed or not, by now you will be at the very least completely buzzed on a caffeine high.

WHERE DOES THE COFFEE CEREMONY ORIGINATE?

It's not surprising that Ethiopia is the home of the coffee ceremony. It's widely recognised as the birthplace of Coffea arabica, a species of coffee plant indigenous to the Ethiopian highlands, and this humble hot brew is at the centre of Ethiopian socialising and culture. It is the country's biggest export, accounting for almost 30 per cent of its annual exports. Ethiopia is the fifth-largest producer of coffee in the world, producing around 2–3 per cent of the world's coffee.

Legend goes that coffee was discovered in the 9th century by a goat-herder named Kaldi after he witnessed the buzzing and energising effects the red berries had after his herd ate them. It's said that Kaldi then tried the fruits for himself and, much like his goats, he was jolted into a hyper state, which he thoroughly enjoyed. The story then goes that Kaldi took them back to his village where he was scolded for partaking of the devil's fruit and they were flung into the fire. Once the tempting aroma of the roasting berries was in the air however, legend has it that the villagers soon changed their minds and, thus, coffee was born.

Coffee shops are found all over Ethiopia today and while in the past few years a number of chain-like coffee shops have sprouted up in the capital, Addis Ababa, the coffee ceremony is still very much a highly valued and important cultural symbol in the country.

WHAT ARE THE HEALTH AND HAPPINESS BENEFITS?

There are many reported health benefits of coffee, but for every benefit there is an equal number of reported negative health effects. So is coffee actually good for you? Caffeine affects everyone differently, but the general consensus is that yes, it can be good for you – if you are able to tolerate it well and as long as it's consumed in moderation.

· Studies suggest that people who drink coffee in moderation are less likely to suffer from cardiovascular disease, heart attacks and stroke, and it may help to prevent Parkinson's disease and type 2 diabetes.
· Coffee is high in antioxidants, thanks to the plant compounds polyphenols.
· Caffeine is a stimulant, which can give you energy, improve mood, alertness and cognitive functions and make you more focused.
· Coffee stimulates the nervous system, which may aid the breakdown of body fat for energy.
· Some reports state that drinking coffee before exercise can improve athletic performance by as much as 10 per cent.
· Negative effects associated with coffee include: insomnia, dizziness, tremors, acid reflux and irregular heartbeat.

The coffee ceremony also contributes to happiness and wellbeing by bringing people together; it's the perfect opportunity for families, friends and neighbours to get together and catch up. The ceremony is a time-honoured tradition and one that cannot be rushed. By taking part you allow yourself to free your mind of any worries or stresses, you get to laugh and communicate with people close to you, and reset and refresh for the rest of the day.

COFFEE CEREMONY | ETHIOPIA

WHERE IN ETHIOPIA CAN I EXPERIENCE THE COFFEE CEREMONY?

The Ethiopian highlands are home to a number of coffee plantations where it's possible to arrange tours and experience the ritual of the coffee ceremony firsthand. If you don't have time to head to the highlands and take part in a coffee ceremony, you can still be treated to an incredible brew and savour the experience in Addis Ababa. The city is full of cafes and coffeehouses, and some of the best coffee in Ethiopia can be found at the following spots.

TOMOCA

Established in 1953 by an Italian owner, Tomoca is well known for serving up some of the capital's best coffee and is decked out with wood-panelled walls and counters lined with coffee-making equipment. Perch yourself on a high stool or find a spot at a standing table to kick off your day with a well-made coffee. They roast their beans onsite and you can pick up a bag to recreate the Ethiopian coffee experience back home. There are several locations around town but the original is in the Piazza neighbourhood.
See: tomocacoffee.com

GALANI CAFE

Galani is a cafe, art gallery and shop and serves some of the most delicious coffee in town, from single-origin beans to seasonal blends, in a spacious, industrial-style setting with concrete floors and comfortable armchairs. You can grab a bag of their beans too, along with some of their organic honey. They also host regular events and workshops, including cupping sessions.
See: galanicoffee.com

KAFA COFFEE MUSEUM

To find out all about coffee production and its history, visit Ethiopia's first coffee museum, which is part of the Kafa Biosphere Reserve in the coffee heartland of the Western Highlands. You'll get a fascinating history lesson on Ethiopian coffee production here.
See: kafa-biosphere.com/coffee-museum

HOW CAN I MAKE THE COFFEE CEREMONY PART OF MY DAILY LIFE AT HOME?

If you're someone who's used to having your thermos coffee in the car on the way to work or school drop-off, grabbing a quick take-away latte or knocking back an espresso as you head out the door, then the first step is learning to change your habit. To try the coffee ceremony in your daily life doesn't mean you have to set aside three hours a day to strictly follow the traditional Ethiopian ceremony, it just means slowing down and appreciating the experience a little more.

CHANGE YOUR COFFEE-MAKING METHODS

If your current coffee set-up is scooping some instant coffee into boiling water or squeezing a pod through a machine, then you could try savouring the experience more by researching some different coffee-making methods. Some suggestions are the V60 pourover, French press, siphon (if you're really serious), and a nice-looking Chemex.

Opt for good-quality, single-origin beans from a local roaster and choose fair-trade and organic where possible – if your budget allows.

Buy yourself a hand-grinder and grind the beans yourself each morning. This task takes a few minutes and can be quite a mindful and meditative task to start the day, not to mention a solid workout for your arm that will have you looking like Popeye in no time.

To slow things down even more you could try a drip-filter as your brewing method. Enjoy the task of pouring water over the ground beans to let them bloom first, then wait 30 seconds before topping up the water and letting the coffee brew over five minutes or so.

MAKE YOUR OWN COFFEE CEREMONY

Make it your daily ritual to sit down at your dining table, kitchen bench, outdoors in your garden, or anywhere away from your desk in the office – wherever makes you feel calm – and really savour the taste. Resist the temptation to grab a take-away on the run, try putting your phone down and really being in the moment. These ideas will really help you enjoy your coffee ceremony:

· Catch up with friends and family and chat over coffee.
· Pop on some music to listen to as you wait while your coffee brews.
· Light some incense to really get into the coffee ceremony vibe.
· Use stylish coffee cups that you enjoy looking at and drinking from each day, to make it that bit more special.

CRYSTAL AND STONE HEALING

USA AND CANADA

WHAT IS CRYSTAL AND STONE HEALING?

There's a current resurgence in the West of the New Age '70s trend of crystal healing. Type it into a search engine and thousands of pages come up, look up the hashtag #crystals on Instagram and you'll find over 10 million posts. The beauty and wellness industry has, in recent years, fuelled a huge demand for crystals and gemstones for healing. While crystal healing has been commercialised by celebrity endorsements, wellness bloggers and influencers, people have been using precious and semi-precious stones and crystals for spiritual, mental and physical healing for thousands of years.

A diverse group of cultures across the globe has used crystals to cure an assortment of ailments, to protect against disease, to help the mind and for spiritual purposes – from the Ancient Sumerians, Egyptians, Greeks, Indians and Chinese to the First Nations people of North America, particularly the Apache and Cherokee tribes. Each tribe has its own set of traditions, rituals and teachings handed down from generation to generation, and different ways in which they use stones and crystals for healing.

Many Native American traditions have been co-opted by New Age health practitioners, including sweat lodges, medicine wheels, dreamcatchers, and crystal and stone healing, but all of these have roots in Indigenous cultural practices. Sweat lodges are a purifying ritual and it's thought that the heat can aid in detoxifying the body by sweating out any impurities, and are used by many tribes across North America, including the Cherokee. Medicine wheels or 'sacred circles' represent the alignment and interaction of the mental, physical and spiritual elements and the belief that life happens in cycles or circles. Dreamcatchers have caught on in mainstream society as a popular wall decoration, but the tradition of these among the Ojibwe people was using them as a talisman to protect sleeping people – especially children. They were believed to filter out bad dreams and only allow good thoughts to enter the mind.

Proponents of crystal healing believe that crystals are a source of energy, that they are very much alive and should be deeply respected. The stones and crystals act as conduits for healing by flowing positive energy into a person's body and the body releases the negative energy into the stone.

WHERE DOES CRYSTAL AND STONE HEALING ORIGINATE?

Many cultures have used crystals and stones since ancient times but the first historical reference is typically credited to the Ancient Sumerians, a civilization founded in the Mesopotamia region, c 4500 BCE.

The Ancient Egyptians used crystals such as lapis lazuli, carnelian and quartz in a number of traditions and ceremonies – from burying the dead to wearing the crystals as jewellery for protection.

Crystals and stones such as sapphires have long been used in India as a way to heal emotional imbalances and in healing practices such as Ayurveda where they are used to balance the doshas (energy or life forces).

Jade has held a significant place in Chinese healing since ancient times and is considered to have strong powers for healing ailments, particularly relating to the kidneys. Crystals and stones are incorporated in traditional Chinese medicine and healing such as in the practice of acupuncture, which sometimes involves the use of crystal-tipped needles.

In Ancient Greece, crystals and stones were believed to have several healing and protective properties. The iron ore hematite produces a blood-red colour when oxidised and the Ancient Greeks associated this with the god of war, Ares. Soldiers would use hematite to rub over their armour before battles to protect themselves.

And of course, crystal and stone healing has been a part of Native American culture for thousands of years, particularly in the Cherokee and Apache tribes, where the rituals and traditions have been passed down by word-of-mouth.

WHAT ARE THE HEALTH AND HAPPINESS BENEFITS?

Debate runs hot over whether there is any substance to claims that crystal healing works. However, believers in crystal and stone healing observe many real benefits.

AGATE

Agate is a variety of microcrystalline quartz and takes on an array of colours and patterns. It's known for its soothing and protecting properties and as a grounding stone that can help create balance, concentration and harmony in your life. It's also said to enhance cognitive function and help in healing the eyes and lymphatic system and in strengthening blood vessels.

CALCITE

Calcite is a rock-forming carbonate mineral and is typically white or clear but can also be grey, brown, orange or yellow. It's considered to be a powerful cleanser of negative energy and believers think that calcite can improve kidney function and strengthen bones and joints.

AMETHYST

Another variety of quartz, amethyst is a popular purple stone and is believed to be a powerful stone for use in protection against negative energy. It's said to relieve stress and bring a sense of contentment, as well as to have a sobering effect to counteract overindulgence in alcohol, food and drugs. Amethyst is also used to relieve insomnia and to enhance sweet dreams by placing it under a person's pillow.

BLOODSTONE

A member of the chalcedony family, bloodstone is a type of quartz, also known as heliotrope, and has a dark green base with spots of bright red through it. It's believed to have blood-purifying properties, helpful for treating anaemia, and to increase creativity and courage. It is also thought to reduce irritability and aggression.

CARNELIAN

This gemstone is another variety of chalcedony and is usually glassy and translucent with a reddish-brown colour. It's used to stimulate energy and creativity and to help calm anger and get rid of negative emotions. Carnelian is also used to give confidence and help the wearer trust their own instincts. It's used to treat back problems and believed to aid in healing the ligaments.

JADE

Jade is two kinds of metamorphic rock – jadeite and nephrite – and it can range from creamy white to emerald green. It's used as a protective stone and a symbol of purity and wisdom. It's thought to increase love and nurturing and to help the wearer become who they really are. It's used to aid in removing toxins and to help with kidney issues, as well as with fertility and childbirth.

QUARTZ

Quartz is a mineral that is found in many rocks and is the most abundant mineral found on the Earth's surface. Pure quartz is clear or white and the word comes from the Greek word for 'ice'. It has a reputation as a 'master healer', as it's thought to amplify energy by absorbing, storing, releasing and regulating it, and is believed to be able to heal a host of ailments while clearing the mind of negative thoughts and emotions.

HOW CAN I MAKE CRYSTAL AND STONE HEALING PART OF MY DAILY LIFE AT HOME?

There are plenty of people claiming to be healers. Be sure to do your research before trying any out.

Unfortunately, as the practice of crystal healing has become more popular and the demand for stones has grown, creating a massive global commercial market, it has had several negative impacts, including environmental damage, poor working conditions for miners and child labour exploitation. Sourcing stones and crystals ethically is a huge challenge for the industry as it's often very difficult to trace the origins of the crystals, as many are mined as a by-product of large-scale mining for other commodities, such as diamonds. Try to buy from places that can tell you how they source their crystals and stones ethically – from small-scale mining sources.

Jade is a popular choice to place in the entrance of a home for its protective properties and is used to encourage wealth and good luck.

If you struggle with getting a good night's sleep you can place amethyst under your pillow, or – if you find that a little too lumpy – on your bedside table. The bedroom is also a great spot to place a bowl of rose quartz, which is used to promote a loving, happy energy in the room.

DOLCE FAR NIENTE

ITALY

WHAT IS DOLCE FAR NIENTE?

Anyone who has been fortunate enough to visit Italy won't be surprised to hear that the concept of dolce far niente – the sweetness of doing nothing – is as Italian as Vespas and pizza. This is a country whose identity is rooted in beauty, fashion, art and gastronomy, with residents who know how to live life and how to live it well. Italians have respect for the finer things in life and take pleasure in everyday activities, from long family lunches and a neighbourhood stroll to a chat at a bar over a piping hot espresso or three, four, five …

Doing nothing is harder than it sounds, though. It feels like a total luxury that isn't realistic for many of us, and a romantic notion that is impossible to carry out in these modern, busy times. Of course, we all (yes, even Italians) have to get our daily duties done. But this concept is not just accessible to the lucky few – dolce far niente is a part of Italian culture and doesn't imply laziness but instead refers to the simple pleasures of relaxing, taking time out and doing sweet nothing. It's a part of everyday life, whether it's sitting on a park bench in a piazza and watching the world go by, enjoying the sunset with an aperitivo (pre-dinner drink) or taking

an evening stroll after dinner. It's a simple concept but one loaded with importance that is truly embraced by Italians and ingrained in the national psyche.

No one is suggesting we all abandon our jobs and responsibilities to sit around sipping wine in the sun all day, every day – as lovely as that sounds. Dolce far niente is simply a way of switching off and being in the moment, truly in the moment, free from distractions and enjoying the pleasure of idleness. It's a precious break from your day. It's about striving for a better work-life balance. It's sitting with friends or family, sharing a meal together, watching the world go by and taking the time to slow down.

WHERE DOES DOLCE FAR NIENTE ORIGINATE?

The term dolce far niente (the sweetness of doing nothing) has Latin roots – dulcis means 'sweet', facere means 'to make or do', and 'nec entem' translates literally as 'not a being'.

The phrase gained some fame outside of Italy thanks to the film *Eat, Pray, Love*, based on Elizabeth Gilbert's novel. In one of the scenes, Julia Roberts's character is being told off by an Italian man in a barber shop about Americans not knowing how to really live and to experience pleasure, and another Italian man chimes in to explain this Italian concept of dolce far niente.

In a country blessed with an unfair amount of spectacular scenery – snow-capped mountains as mere backdrops to impossibly charming villages; vineyard-laced, emerald-carpeted hills; craggy coastlines lapped by turquoise waters; and cities of architectural splendour – it's little wonder Italians like to take a break every now and then to simply sit back and lap it all up.

WHAT ARE THE HEALTH AND HAPPINESS BENEFITS?

It's almost impossible for many of us to consider doing absolutely nothing. It feels like we're doing something wrong, like we're being lazy, unproductive, slobbish even! We find ourselves sitting down trying to take a break or relax and our mind kicks into gear automatically: 'I better see whose doing what on social media', 'I need to finish that TV series before my free online streaming trial expires', 'I should be repainting the kitchen right now'. We don't freely allow ourselves the chance to just be idle, to let our brains fully rest and to take pleasure in it, but in doing so we can reap a number of benefits. If the idea of doing nothing doesn't do it for you, here are some of the potential health and wellness benefits:

- It helps the mind and body recharge the batteries and reset, avoiding burnout from too much stress.
- Studies suggest that taking time to do nothing can boost your creativity and problem-solving skills, as it clears up space in the subconscious.
- Disconnecting from our phones and technology helps us reconnect to the real world, to nature and to other people.
- We can improve our mental health by giving our brain some downtime. The act of just being alone with our thoughts also helps us tune into our emotions and to find out what's really going on with ourselves, what we're feeling and how we're coping. By keeping busy all the time we can miss out on vital clues.

WHERE IN ITALY CAN I EXPERIENCE DOLCE FAR NIENTE?

The home of dolce far niente offers countless opportunities and scenarios for indulging in the sweetness of doing nothing. From admiring a beautiful villa garden to sitting back and watching the waves lapping the sands of a rocky beach. From sitting outside a restaurant in a piazza enjoying an aperitivo (pre-dinner drink) to sampling homemade gelato flavours while exploring a city. If you want to live la dolce vita (the good life) like an Italian, here are some great spots for experiencing dolce far niente.

VILLA CARLOTTA

There are far worse places to do nothing than on the shores of Lake Como. If you find soaking up the stupendous views of the sweeping lake, mountains and postcard-perfect villages too dull, then you can head to the spectacular botanical garden of Villa Carlotta on the lake's shore. The garden bursts with colour over 8 hectares (19 acres), and there's even a Zen rock garden to help you with your pursuit of relaxation.
See: villacarlotta.it

ROME'S PIAZZAS

Do as the locals do and take a break with the added entertainment of people watching thrown in at Rome's piazzas. Piazza Navona is the standout square in the centre of the city with its elegant palaces and grand, decorative fountains, along with street artists. For the ultimate in people watching, the Spanish Steps at Piazza di Spagna is where you'll want to seat yourself. The 135 steps take you from the square up to the Chiesa della Trinità dei Monti, where you can take in the incredible views over Rome. But you can always claim you're indulging in dolce far niente if you can't be bothered climbing up.

AMALFI COAST

More eye-popping views await along Italy's most famous coastline, the Amalfi Coast. Here you have plenty of opportunities for staring out at the tempting blue sea and gorgeous sun-drenched villages. Bored yet? Didn't think so.

VENICE

This magical floating city attracts tourists by the boat-loads and for good reason. Sure, you can admire artworks at the Gallerie dell'Accademia or the Peggy Guggenheim Collection, but this city is a masterpiece all of its own. The beauty of spending time here is simply sitting in the Piazza San Marco and taking in the grandeur of the architecture around you and envying the lifestyle of Venetians, or wandering the maze of backstreets and stopping at the peak of a bridge to watch gondolas glide beneath, navigating narrow canals.

TUSCANY

Tuscany is famous for its idyllic scenery of undulating hills, vineyards, olive groves and charming hilltop villages. You can travel from the medieval towers of San Gimignano to the red city of Siena and the Renaissance jewel of Florence. Along the way, take in vineyard views, cellar doors and quaint villages or stand in front of an awe-inspiring artwork in Florence's Uffizi. Wherever you are, be sure to take a break and drink in the views around you or indulge in a spot of aimless wandering before heading back to your villa to take a not-at-all earned nap. Dolce far niente.

HOW CAN I MAKE DOLCE FAR NIENTE PART OF MY DAILY LIFE AT HOME?

Do you look at your daily list of tasks in the morning and wish you could stay in bed under the covers? Does your commute in heavy traffic or elbowing passengers on a train have you longing for a few hours of quiet time for yourself? When you get home from work or study exhausted, do you still have to cook dinner, tidy the house, take a conference call or do the washing? Don't you sometimes wish you could just do nothing? That's where the Italians have it all figured out with dolce far niente. It's genius.

How could you benefit by getting off the constant treadmill of schedules, appointments, tasks, chores, social media and events and just literally watch the paint dry or the grass grow for a bit instead?

DITCH THE GUILT

There tends to be a lot of guilt associated with doing nothing and it's increasingly becoming the case that relentless pressure is put on us, by ourselves and by others, to feel that being constantly busy is a sign of success. Stop worrying about what others might think. Stop pressuring yourself to be constantly busy. This is the first step to being able to enjoy the art of doing nothing.

PUT DOWN THE PHONE

We associate doing nothing with scrolling on our smartphones and other devices without purpose. Most of us have forgotten what it's like to be alone with our thoughts, to just sit and be. But what would it feel like to really do nothing, without the comfort of your phone or device to entertain you? This might be the toughest thing for many of us to get used to but you can't be doing nothing when you are connected to technology. Disconnect. Turn off the TV and put your phone, laptop or tablet out of reach. Start off by doing it for 15 minutes,

then 30, then a few hours and see if you can work up to a full day without constantly checking social media.

SIT STILL AND JUST BE

Curl up on an armchair and stare out the window. Grab a spot on your balcony and look out at the street below. Lie down on a picnic blanket and gaze up at the clouds. Pop on some soothing music and sit and listen to it. Just try to get comfortable not fidgeting, not needing to be doing something and just being alone with your thoughts. Many of us don't get the chance very often, so savour it for as long as you can.

LEAVE IT

The dishes, that email, the laundry. Whatever it might be, it can wait a while. Try not to get caught up in needing to tick everything off your list all the time. If the dishes don't get done until the morning, it's okay. Prioritise your downtime – even if you have to schedule it in initially, until it becomes part of your normal habits.

FIKA

SWEDEN

WHAT IS FIKA?

Put simply, fika (pronounced feeka) is a coffee break that usually involves having a cup of coffee, or tea, paired with a pastry. Bonus! Though the relative simplicity of the activity belies its importance in Swedish culture. This coffee break is considered a daily necessity and is an integral part of Swedish social life.

Fika is not just about sitting down to enjoy a hot brew, it's a way of taking time out of your day for a break, to slow down and connect. You can take a fika break alone or with friends, family or colleagues. It can be done in a cafe, at home, at work or in a park. Sweden is a large consumer of coffee – Scandinavian countries top the list globally of the number of cups of coffee consumed per day, per capita, so it's no surprise coffee is a feature of fika. But tea is just as acceptable in a fika break. When it comes to fika, the details don't really matter. What's important is the escape from your busy routine and daily life demands, to sit by yourself reflecting and clearing the mind, or to connect with people in your life, chatting and catching up.

WHERE DOES FIKA ORIGINATE?

Ska vi fika? (Should we fika?) – a phrase as quintessentially Swedish as IKEA and ABBA. Fika is a long-held tradition in Sweden and though the exact beginning of it is largely unknown, it's thought to have started as early as 1913. The word fika comes from the old Swedish word for coffee 'kaffi' and reversing the parts and slightly altering the word to make fika.

In many countries, coffee tends to lean more towards a 'grab and go' culture. Whether that's having a few scalding gulps of coffee made at home before rushing out the door to work or to drop the kids at school, or squeezing in the time to grab a take-away from a local cafe on your lunch break. Fika is the opposite of this. It's about treating your coffee break as an important moment to take time out for yourself. Unlike in a lot of Western countries, you won't see many people with laptops working at cafes in Sweden. It's more about seeing friends and having a chat or sitting quietly reading – it's about savouring the present moment.

Fika is not forgotten about at the Swedish workplace, either. Most office spaces and companies have a fika room, where workers can take a proper break instead of having coffee or lunch at their desk. It provides a dedicated place to take time away from the computer screen, to chat or simply clear your mind of your work for a while. It's well known that Swedish businesses believe that fika increases productivity, efficiency and the general wellbeing of employees, and sometimes colleagues will bring in home-baked cakes and cookies to share for fika at work.

WHAT ARE THE HEALTH AND HAPPINESS BENEFITS?

Sweden is known for having some of the happiest residents in the world and consistently ranks high on the annual World Happiness Report, so there's got to be something to this fika culture, right? Taking a dedicated break has several health and happiness benefits.

INCREASES PRODUCTIVITY

Taking time to pause from your work or daily tasks might sound counterintuitive to increasing your productivity, but this can actually lead to a boost in productivity, along with an increase in your general happiness and wellbeing. That's why so many of Sweden's top companies require employees to take two fika breaks a day, in the morning and in the afternoon.

IMPROVES CONCENTRATION

Many studies show that just by taking a short 15-minute break from your work can refresh the mind and help you stay focused and avoid burnout.

HELPS FOSTER RELATIONSHIPS

Sitting down for a coffee and a chat at work can lead to more effective working relationships with colleagues. Fika can help to develop deeper and more meaningful friendships.

BETTER MENTAL HEALTH

By avoiding burning yourself out and giving your mind the time to rest and reset, your mental health will improve. And fostering better relationships is another big tick for a healthy mind and mental wellbeing.

WHERE IN SWEDEN CAN I EXPERIENCE FIKA?

You'll find plenty of fika opportunities throughout Sweden and in hundreds of cafes in Stockholm alone, whether you're after a cosy traditional coffeehouse or a modern, hip boutique cafe. The traditional place to engage in a bit of fika in Sweden is a konditori, a sort of combination of a coffeehouse and patisserie, serving a range of tea, coffee and pastries.

ROSENDALS TRÄDGÅRDSKAFE, STOCKHOLM

Rosendals is a gorgeous setting for a fika break, located in the sanctuary of the botanical gardens. The garden cafe uses organic and biodynamic produce grown onsite and there is a bakery next door where you can pick up freshly baked bread, pastries and preserves to take home or to your accommodation. In the summer months, you can sit down on the grass between the orchards and soak up the sun. See: rosendalstradgard.se/in-english

VETE-KATTEN, STOCKHOLM

Cosy into a back table in this charmingly old-world Stockholm institution, around since the 1920s. The delightful maze of nooks and crannies are laced with the aroma of fresh cinnamon and cardamom buns. If you're after a more substantial bite with your coffee, it also does heaving sandwiches. See: vetekatten.se/en

GRILLSKA HUSETS KONDITORI, STOCKHOLM

Located in the cobblestoned historic Gamla Stan square in the heart of Stockholm's Old Town, this bakery beckons with its tempting aroma of baked treats. The streetside terrace is the perfect fika spot when the sun's out.

HOW CAN I MAKE FIKA PART OF MY DAILY LIFE AT HOME?

Most of us would already be taking a coffee or tea break here and there in our daily lives, so taking an extra step to turn it into a fika break should not be too much of a stretch. The main change may be simply your attitude towards that tea or coffee break and making it a more mindful experience.

FIKA AT WORK

If you're at work and you usually quickly make your hot brew in the break room or kitchen and rush it back to your desk to continue working, then first you'll need to change this up.

Find yourself a quiet spot to sit with your drink so you're escaping the work environment for 10 to 15 minutes. Think about non-work things, such as what your plans are for the weekend, what you would like to cook for dinner that night, what your family and friends might be up to. Let your mind drift away so you can return to your work feeling refreshed and renewed. If you prefer a little company, ask a co-worker or two to join you for a chat while you have your tea or coffee. You could even introduce bringing home-baked goods into work and share them with your colleagues.

FIKA AT HOME

If you're at home the same general idea applies. Don't gulp down your drink in between stacking the dishwasher, sitting in front of the TV, folding the laundry or feeding the kids. Make it a dedicated break. Catch some sun in the garden while you sip your morning coffee,

sit by the window with a tea in the afternoon and reflect on your day, or head to a local cafe with a friend and really catch up on what's going on in your lives.

When entertaining friends at home for fika, it's a nice idea to serve your tea and snacks using lovely teacups and saucers and have everything beautifully presented to show the importance of fika to Swedish culture.

BAKING GOODS

Now snacks to accompany fika are serious stuff in Sweden. There is a broad range of mostly baked goods and pastries the Swedes love to indulge in, and a number of classic traditional recipes that are often used. Some of the favourites include kanelbullar (cinnamon buns, see p.39) and kardemummabullar (cardamom buns). The love for kanelbullar is such that Sweden even has a national day dedicated to the cinnamon bun on 4 October! Fika can also become a quick meal, replacing the baked goods and pastries with open-faced sandwiches called smörgås. You can bake your own treats or buy from a bakery.

What you choose to eat during fika is not really that important, though home-baked goods are usually preferred. The importance is placed on the activity itself – the interaction with loved ones or colleagues and giving your mind a bit of a rest. And if you're not much of a baker, never mind, hit up your local IKEA – they usually sell pre-baked frozen cinnamon buns!

Cinnamon buns (kanelbullar)

MAKES 20

DOUGH

55G/2 OZ UNSALTED BUTTER
200ML/7 FL. OZ/1 CUP MILK
1 X 7G/2 TSP SACHET OF DRIED YEAST
375G/13 OZ/3 CUPS PLAIN FLOUR
2 TBSP BROWN SUGAR
55G/2 OZ CASTER SUGAR
¼ TSP SALT
1 TSP GROUND CARDAMOM

FILLING

55G/2 OZ SOFTENED UNSALTED BUTTER
45G/1.5 OZ BROWN SUGAR
1 TBSP CINNAMON

TO DECORATE

1 EGG, BEATEN
PEARL SUGAR (OPTIONAL)
FLAKED ALMONDS (OPTIONAL)

1. To make the dough, melt the butter in a large saucepan and then add the milk and heat to a light boil. Remove from the heat and let cool (so it's warm to touch) and stir in the yeast until it has dissolved.

2. In a large mixing bowl combine the flour, sugars, salt and cardamom. Make a well in the middle and pour in the wet ingredients. Mix with a wooden spoon until you have rough dough.

3. Turn the dough onto a clean surface and knead for around 5 minutes. Add a little flour if the dough is a bit too sticky. Once you have your dough ready, transfer to a floured bowl and cover with cling wrap and a clean tea towel. Place the bowl in a dark, warm spot to let it rise for around 45 minutes.

4. Preheat the oven to 220°C /430°F.

5. To prepare the filling, beat together the butter, brown sugar and cinnamon in a bowl until it resembles a smooth paste.

6. Once your dough has risen, punch it down in the bowl and cut the dough in half. Roll one of the halves out into a rectangle around 3mm thick and spread half of the filling over it.

7. Starting with the long edge of your dough, roll up the dough tightly, creating a snail effect and then slice the dough log into 10 pieces. Repeat steps 6 and 7 with the other half of the dough.

8. Place the pieces face up on a baking sheet lined with baking paper and brush the buns with beaten egg. Sprinkle with pearl sugar and flaked almonds, if using.

9. Place the baking sheet in the oven and reduce the heat to 190°C /375°F and bake for around 10 to 15 minutes or until golden brown.

INTERVIEW

Anna Brones

Swedish–American freelance writer and artist Anna Brones, co-author of *Fika: The Art of the Swedish Coffee Break* (2015).

WHAT ARE YOUR FAVOURITE PLACES TO ENGAGE IN FIKA?

I personally love fika outside. Whether that means going on a bike ride and packing a thermos of coffee and a treat, or just taking my coffee break outside my house on a sunny day.

WHAT SNACKS ARE YOUR GO-TO WHEN ENJOYING A FIKA BREAK?

My favorite fika item is a cardamom bun, but I don't make them that often. They are an extra special treat. I also like chokladbollar, which are chocolate balls made with butter and oats. Those are pretty simple to make, so it's an easy recipe when you're craving a fika treat in a pinch.

WHAT ARE THE MAIN HAPPINESS AND WELLBEING BENEFITS OF TAKING A FIKA BREAK?

I think that taking time for fika means taking time to have a break from the routine. It's not coffee consumed while sitting in front of your computer and scrolling through a newsfeed.

Fika is often social, so it's a nice time to just sit and be with friends, but it can also be done alone. I think it's important for our wellbeing to have time where we are just in the present. Not focusing on what we need to do, or what's on the schedule, just a little moment where our minds can wander and we can find contentment where we are.

FRILUFTSLIV

NORWAY

WHAT IS FRILUFTSLIV?

It's widely known that the Scandinavian countries consistently place in the top ranks when it comes to the World Happiness Report – and Norway is no exception. Part of this happiness comes down to a Norwegian term that is not easy to translate but loosely means 'free air life'. Friluftsliv, pronounced free-loofts-leev, refers to an outdoor lifestyle and Norwegians' love of nature and getting out into the wild. Importantly, the concept also means enjoying nature without disturbing or damaging it – engaging with it with deep respect.

Friluftsliv is integral to Norwegian culture and society. If you don't like the outdoors, you basically have no business being in Norway! What might be considered a casual weekend activity in other countries is treated as religion in Norway – Norwegians' passion for outdoor activities and getting back to nature is part of their character. Children are taught from a very young age how to interact with nature, as well as outdoor activities such as skiing and survival skills. But friluftsliv doesn't mean the same thing to everyone. It can range from an extreme week-long glacier hike or a hardcore skiing expedition, to an easy hike in the forest with a friend or relaxing in an outdoor sauna by a lake.

Norway even has a law for it. The Right to Roam under the *Outdoor Recreation Act* 1957 states that anyone has permission to roam freely in the outdoors and to camp anywhere, as long as they show respect and care for the environment. In other words, leave things as you found them and don't cause any damage to nature. This law is based on an ancient right called allemannsretten (everyman's right).

I hear you say: 'But isn't it too ridiculously cold in Norway for all this outdoor business?' Yes … yes, it mostly is. But in Norway, this excuse won't fly. Snow, ice, glaciers – what the rest of us might consider deterrents to going outside, Norwegians consider great reasons for going outside! Rather than complaining about the weather or using it as an excuse, it is embraced and appreciated.

WHERE DOES FRILUFTSLIV ORIGINATE?

The concept of friluftsliv has been part of Norwegian culture for centuries but Norwegian playwright Henrik Ibsen first popularised the term in 1859 in a poem called *On the Heights*.

Perhaps the Norwegians' intrinsic passion for nature can be attributed to its accessibility. This is a country of breathtaking beauty where snow blankets the stunning scenery made up of grand glaciers, rugged forests and fjords flanked by incredibly steep sides.

WHAT ARE THE HEALTH AND HAPPINESS BENEFITS?

REDUCES STRESS

When you leave the house and head into the outdoors, you are making a step to disconnect from your busy and preoccupied life. It's a way of escaping whatever it is that might be causing you worry, tension or stress. You get to leave that all behind for a while to focus on yourself and the natural world around you. This helps calm the mind and body and reduce stress levels.

BOOSTS CREATIVITY AND PRODUCTIVITY

Being out in nature helps to clear the mind and to reset. You give your mind the chance to slow down and think more carefully. Nature can improve your mood and wellbeing through fresh air and this in turn can help boost creativity or productivity at work or at home. Having a bit of a break can help you avoid burnout and get you back to performing at your best.

HELPS STRENGTHEN RELATIONSHIPS

For many Norwegians, friluftsliv is about not just spending time in nature alone, but often as the main social activity with friends and family. Weekend hikes, ski trips and ice-fishing are all ways that people can spend time together in the outdoors, and this helps cultivate relationships and ways to bond together. You're spending quality time away from the normal stresses you might have at home, like trying to get housework or homework done.

REDUCES THE RISK OF ILLNESS AND DISEASE

Many studies have shown that exposure to nature and the outdoors can help with everything from reducing cardiovascular disease and the risk of type 2 diabetes to lowering blood pressure and overall boosting the immune system.

BUILDS RESILIENCE AND CHARACTER

Being in nature can take you out of your comfort zone and challenge you, particularly for Norwegians who love to engage in extreme outdoor adventures such as ice-climbing, glacier kayaking or even reindeer sledding! By challenging yourself, taking risks and trying something new in what might be tough conditions, you build resilience, courage and mental strength.

IMPROVES SLEEP AND MOOD

We all know that blissful sleep after a full day out in the fresh air. Nature helps relax us and calm the mind, the first step to getting a good night's sleep. Exposure to natural light, away from the artificial lighting of our home or office, may help to regulate our body clocks, too.

WHERE IN NORWAY CAN I EXPERIENCE FRILUFTSLIV?

Friluftsliv is everywhere in Norway, thanks to its incredible landscape and number of national parks dotting the country; it's a dream destination for anyone keen to explore the outdoors. There's no shortage of summer hiking and walking trails and plenty of winter activities, too. Most Norwegians live in close proximity to nature and even in Oslo it's easy to escape the city and be in the forest in less than half an hour.

JOTUNHEIMEN NATIONAL PARK

This national park is home to 60 glaciers and the highest peak in Norway, Galdhøpiggen. The name translates as 'Home of the Giants' and as you hike the trails in the shadows of some 200 mountains, you'll know why. One of the most popular hikes here is the Besseggen ridge. It's an incredibly beautiful park and a must-visit for outdoor enthusiasts.

PREIKESTOLEN

Preikestolen (Pulpit Rock) is one of the most iconic landmarks in Norway. The rock perches dramatically on a sheer cliff above the waters of Lysefjord. It involves a two-hour hike to reach it – child's play for Norwegians – and is well worth it as it provides some of the most stunning scenic views in the country.

DOG-SLEDDING

A quintessential Arctic experience on a sled being pulled by a team of huskies is where you'll get to see the real wilderness in Karasjok in Norway's far north. You can opt for a casual few hours on the sled or go more hardcore with multi-day trips.

SKIING, LILLEHAMMER REGION

Norway has some of the best skiing in the world with plenty of powder, thanks to its long winter season. There are hundreds of ski resorts across the country offering downhill and cross-country skiing, but the Lillehammer region is the top pick, with not one but two Olympic slopes – Hafjell and Kvitjell.

SNOWMOBILING, SVALBARD

If you're no snow bunny and your skiing style is more splits than shredding, never fear, you can still get out on the snow without making a fool of yourself or doing an injury. Swap the skis for a snowmobile ride to experience Norway's icy Arctic wilderness in Svalbard. This way you'll get to explore deeper into the natural scenery and reach higher parts of the mountains. All without having to wear out your legs, too!

HOW CAN I MAKE FRILUFTSLIV PART OF MY DAILY LIFE AT HOME?

Don't have majestic fjords on your doorstep? No huskies pulling sleds around your neighbourhood? Don't worry. You can incorporate the concept of fruliftsliv into your life even if you're not fortunate enough to live in Norway's knockout natural surroundings. It's about getting outdoors and into nature. By the time many of us have made it to the weekend after an exhausting week of work and looking after the kids, we might be tempted to order pizza with a glass of wine and lie on the couch indoors streaming TV. And while this is great every now and then, take a leaf out of the Norwegians' book and break the habit and get back to nature. Anyone can do it. It's just a matter of choice.

SWAP THE GYM

If your exercise routine usually involves running on a treadmill at the gym, swap this out for a run outdoors instead. Find a local running track, a nearby park, a forest trail, or even just the streets around your neighbourhood if you don't have access to nature close by.

GO FOR A WALK

It couldn't be easier. If you're not one for extreme adventures or anything too physically demanding, just going for a walk is a low-impact way of getting some physical activity outside. And again, it's best to find a peaceful spot somewhere in nature, but if you can't manage that, just make do with what you have. If you were planning on driving to the shops, walk instead. If you usually sit at your desk for lunch, go for a walk after you've eaten. If you were going to drive to pick up the kids from school, walk instead and all walk home together.

HAVE A PICNIC

Grab a bunch of friends or your family and organise a picnic day at your local park, river, beach or head to a nature reserve or national park. Or it can be as simple as opting to have your lunch outside, instead of sitting indoors with the TV on or glued to your phone. Set up a picnic blanket in your backyard or set and style the outdoor table and invite a bunch of friends over for a long weekend lunch outside. You can get great ideas for table settings from Pinterest, but then leave your phone inside while you picnic.

WATCH THE SUNRISE OR SUNSET

If you have a favourite viewpoint in your local area, check what time sunrise or sunset is and schedule time to head to that viewpoint and take in the beauty of nature.

EMBRACE THE WEATHER

Ditch the attitude of 'I can't go for that run now as it's raining, or cold or windy', or whatever your excuse is. Make like a Norwegian and embrace it. Rug up, grab an umbrella, pop on your gumboots (wellingtons) and get out there.

START A NEW HOBBY

Find a new hobby that will get you outdoors. If you're someone who needs more motivation to get going, you might find it's much easier to try a new hobby in a group setting. Join an outdoor yoga class or a personal training session outdoors. Start bike-riding or nature photography. Find something you enjoy, otherwise it won't last and you'll be in on the couch again in no time.

GEZELLIGHEID
THE NETHERLANDS

WHAT IS GEZELLIGHEID?

While the wellness world has been obsessed with the Danish concept of hygge (*see* p.64) in recent years, a little-known similar Dutch philosophy has flown under the radar – gezelligheid (try your luck at pronouncing it 'heh-zell-ick'). This Dutch word is untranslatable but has similar sentiments to hygge; it's all about comfort, cosiness, togetherness, contentedness and conviviality. Gezelligheid is a very important part of Dutch culture and social relationships. It is best described as a general feeling, a warm, fuzzy feeling you get from enjoying being with others. Gezelligheid is about taking pleasure in the simple things in life and spending time with loved ones. Who can argue with that?

Simplistically it might be translated as 'cosy', so something gezellig can refer to an inviting restaurant, home, pub or cafe when it's cold and dark outside – a place that beckons with its warmth, soft amber lighting and people socialising. But it can also refer to the act of spending time with the people in our lives and having a fun and relaxed time. So, a cosy cafe or a pub can be gezellig, and catching up with a friend for a picnic in the park can be gezellig, too.

And while you've got gezelligheid, there's also the opposite of it – ongezellig. A doctor's clinic could be ongezellig, for example. Or you might find a cafe or bar not at all inviting, so you could say to your friend, 'Let's go somewhere else, this place is ongezellig'.

WHERE DOES GEZELLIGHEID ORIGINATE?

The word is said to be a derivative of the traditional word 'gezel', which means companion or friend.

Entertaining at home is a popular pastime in the Netherlands, more popular than in a lot of other countries. The Dutch love to invite people to their homes for borrel (drinks) and food. This is considered a very gezellig social activity.

Think Amsterdam's brown cafes (actually pubs), named for the tobacco stains the walls have developed over the centuries, flickering candles and soft lighting. The famous brown cafes are an icon of gezelligheid, steeped in history and found dotted all over the city. The atmosphere is perfectly gezellig, with a cosy feel and a joyous sense of togetherness.

WHAT ARE THE HEALTH AND HAPPINESS BENEFITS?

Spending time with the people we love and who are important to us helps us feel secure and happy. It lifts our mood and relieves stress and anxiety. Connection to people is hugely important for our mental wellbeing. So by having a gezellig experience, you are helping to improve your mental state, and the flow-on benefits that come from that.

WHERE IN THE NETHERLANDS CAN I EXPERIENCE GEZELLIGHEID?

If you have Dutch friends, then you'll probably find yourself lucky enough to be invited to their home for a meal. Here you'll experience true gezelligheid. The ubiquitous brown cafes in Amsterdam are also a good place to start your gezelligheid experience. Grab some friends and find a snug nook for some good conversation, drinks and comfort food. These are some of the standout picks:

IN 'T AEPJEN

A characterful 15th-century wooden building that has been operating as a tavern since 1519. Candles burn day and night to provide the perfect gezellig atmosphere. Try a locally made jenever (Dutch gin) to warm your cockles.

DE SLUYSWACHT

Opposite Rembrandt's house on the canal's edge, this tall, narrow black building was once the lockkeeper's house and the terrace is a fantastic spot to soak up some sun (when it's out) or to peer out at the canal views from the cosy interior. Dig into a plate of the classic Dutch bar snack bitterballen (bite-sized deep-fried meatballs). See: sluyswacht.nl

CAFE HOPPE

Lively crowds mingle out front of this Amsterdam institution, knocking back brews at one of the city's oldest bars. Inside the canal house, the wood-panelled interior and soft decorative lighting sets the mood. See: cafehoppe.com

HOW CAN I MAKE GEZELLIGHEID PART OF MY DAILY LIFE AT HOME?

You don't need much to add a bit of gezelligheid to your life. In fact, you've probably already been experiencing it. Catching up with friends and family at a pub or restaurant, or having friends over for a dinner party with plenty of good food, wine and lively discussion, are some ideas. If you really want to add a Dutch element, make sure you include a few wheels of moreish Dutch cheese. Simply wearing your fluffiest pair of woollen socks while curled up on the couch wrapped in a blanket with an absorbing novel is another idea, or catching up with a friend at a local cafe with the open fire going and sipping on a steaming cup of hot chocolate.

A genuine gezellig atmosphere should be open-minded, relaxed and fun, too. Remember, a person's idea of what gezellig is can be very subjective. For one person it could be walking in the rain, or stroking your cat on your lap, while for others it might be cooking with your loved ones or reading to your children.

If you don't dine at the table regularly and instead sit on the couch to eat while the TV is on, take note that Dutch families make a habit out of gathering around the dining table at a set time each night to chat about their day. Try to make this part of your daily routine with your family, partner or housemate. Perhaps you have a fire-pit in the garden that you can sit around and toast marshmallows, or maybe you can take pillows onto your balcony to create a new cosy space. Try lying in the park looking at the sky with family and friends.

Doing things that make us feel good, cosy and comfortable help us feel connected with each other. It's also a great way of disconnecting from devices, TV, smartphones and social media. Gezellig activities encourage us to be outdoors or to indulge in great food and a warming cup of tea or a relaxing wine. It aids in lowering stress levels and releasing those good old helpful endorphins.

LIGHTING

In order to recreate Dutch gezelligheid at home, first think about the lighting in your home. You want to avoid harsh, bright lighting. Soft lighting helps ramp up that cosy feel. Candles are an easy way to get a gezellig atmosphere going. Dimmer lights also help, as do lamps. Turn off the overhead main lights and opt for a few table lamps and floor lamps to create warmth and ambience.

FLOWERS

Lovely blooms are a great way to make your home more gezellig. Choose whichever flowers take your fancy and pop some in vases or old jam jars around your house. You don't need to spend money on bouquets, rather gather wildflowers or ask a friend if you can pick some foliage from their garden – if you don't have your own. If you have young children, this is a great activity to do with them – get them to arrange leaves or flowers in a bowl.

MATERIALS

Think about warm and moody materials in your furnishings and decor – dark wood and natural textiles are a good place to start. Choose furniture that has character and will age well. Many of us don't have the budget for antiques but you can pick up characterful pieces from secondhand shops, garage sales, car-boot sales or sometimes even roadside. Pieces that tell the story of their provenance are of so much more value than buying new. Plus you're doing our planet a big favour.

GROSS NATIONAL HAPPINESS [GNH]

BHUTAN

WHAT IS GROSS NATIONAL HAPPINESS?

The mystical, tiny and remote kingdom of Bhutan is nestled in the Himalayas with its fluttering prayer flags flying high over valleys, snow-capped mountain peaks, ancient monasteries and majestic forests. It has long been considered a real-life Shangri-La, and most famously for the kingdom's pursuit of happiness and measuring the mood of its residents through Gross National Happiness (GNH).

GNH is rooted in the principles of the country's religion, Buddhism; it values compassion over capitalism and takes a holistic approach to gaining a better understanding of the general wellbeing of Bhutanese citizens. By introducing GNH, Bhutan sought to have a new tool that would be useful for government, businesses and NGOs in regards to policymaking.

GNH was introduced in Bhutan as an alternative to Gross Domestic Product (GDP) in 1972. It was a new and inventive approach to measuring the country's progress and development through tracking the physical, social and environmental health of its people and the natural environment. Since then, Bhutan has become more and more synonymous with happiness, and has become a sort of pilgrimage destination for travellers who want to witness this Shangri-La for themselves.

Owing to its stunning natural beauty, ecotourism is big business in Bhutan. In order to manage this and avoid the pitfalls of overtourism, the nation imposed a tax of US$250 per day, per visitor to offset any damaging environmental impact, which it calls its 'High Value, Low Impact' tourism strategy. In early 2020, Bhutan also introduced a daily US$17 Sustainable Development Fee for all visitors from the neighbouring countries of India, the Maldives and Bangladesh (who are exempt from the US$250 tax) to tackle the sharp rise in the number of visitors from the region and to further protect its environment.

WHERE DOES GNH ORIGINATE?

The fourth King of Bhutan, King Jigme Singye Wangchuck, who ascended the throne in 1972, first coined the term Gross National Happiness (GNH). He declared that Gross Domestic Product (GDP) was not the most effective or meaningful measure for wellbeing, and that GNH was more important as a path to development. The Bhutanese government decided that it was going to reject the idea of GDP and introduce GNH as its measure of progress.

What may have started out as a general philosophy began to become a more concrete and quantifiable measure over the decades that followed. GNH was enshrined in the constitution in 2008, and in 2011 the UN adopted Bhutan's concept for a more holistic approach to see if it can be used more widely as a development indicator, a move which 68 countries endorsed.

The Gross National Happiness Centre considers four key pillars when conducting its surveys to arrive at the Gross National Happiness Index. The first surveys were conducted in 2010 and 2015 and the next one in 2020. The four key pillars are environmental conservation, good governance, sustainable and equitable socio-economic development, and preservation and promotion of culture. These are then broken down further into nine interconnected domains:

1. Living standards
2. Education
3. Health
4. Environment
5. Community vitality
6. Time-use
7. Psychological wellbeing
8. Good governance
9. Cultural resilience and promotion

Questions asked in the survey in the past have included those on the subject of spirituality such as: 'How often do you practice meditation?' and 'How frequently do you pray?' The survey aims to find out how content a person is with their life and what their values might be with questions such as: 'What are the six or seven things that you consider to be most important that leads to a happy and content life?' and 'Do you lose much sleep over worrying about things?' The survey strives to get to the heart of relationships and family life, including personal questions about how well individuals get along with their family members and neighbours.

WHAT ARE THE HEALTH AND HAPPINESS BENEFITS?

All of this surveying, analysing and focusing on citizens' wellbeing must make Bhutan a land of the happiest, smiliest people on Earth, right? Not quite. Bhutan ranked 95th on the World Happiness Report in 2019. The kingdom is constantly facing big challenges, including climate change issues, and remains one of the poorest countries on the planet, with many of its citizens living without electricity.

However, in a region that is well known for conflict, terrorism and unrest, Bhutan continues to be a kingdom of peace with a stable political and economic environment. On the 2019 Global Peace Index, Bhutan moved two places higher to score number 15 out of the 163 countries ranked, recording the largest improvement of any country that made it into the top 20, having risen 43 places in the past 12 years.

According to the World Bank, Bhutan cut its level of poverty by two-thirds in the last decade and it has one of the fastest growing economies in the world (dominated by hydropower), with its average annual growth of Gross Domestic Product (GDP) at 7.5 per cent since the early 1980s, though this did level out a bit in 2018–19 due to a decline in hydropower production.

The Bhutanese have access to free universal health care and the life expectancy has increased from just over 50 to 71 years over the past few decades. Gross National Happiness (GNH) doesn't just focus on the wellbeing of people, but the protection and sustainability of the environment and the natural landscape of

Bhutan is also a key factor in the pillars of GNH. While the rest of the world took decades to catch on and have still been very slow to adapt, Bhutan banned plastic bags back in 1999. It also became the first smoke-free nation when it banned tobacco in 2005.

Its critics have claimed that its strict commitment to preserving its culture – a key pillar of GNH – has led to a kind of 'ethnic cleansing' of its minorities. Critics argue that by adhering to the strict guidelines, the commitment to happiness has not been applied consistently to the country's residents, and has intentionally omitted minority groups and different cultures.

Advocates for GNH argue that it does not guarantee total happiness for the people of Bhutan and to believe so is to miss the point of it entirely. Instead, GNH should be seen as a guiding principle and vision for a path towards a more equitable and sustainable society. The aim of GNH is to show the Bhutanese population's general wellbeing in a more meaningful and accurate way than a purely monetary measure could do.

HOW CAN I MAKE GROSS NATIONAL HAPPINESS (GNH) PART OF MY DAILY LIFE AT HOME?

While you might not live in a country that's about to ditch its GDP for GNH, there are lessons to be learnt from Bhutan's approach and things you can easily do in your daily life to help guide you on a similar path. It's about re-evaluating what's important to you and trying to shift from a capitalist, consumerist attitude or habit into a more holistic mindset.

LIVE WITH MORE COMPASSION

If a conflict arises or someone aggravates you, try to put yourself in the other person's shoes. Let your ego go and rise above it and let compassion and kindness guide your actions.

SHIFT FROM A MATERIALISTIC MINDSET

Recognise that status and wealth are not the ultimate paths to happiness. Shuffle your priorities around if necessary and work out what makes you happy – not who or what you are trying to compete with or keep up with in society. Focus on what gives you enjoyment.

SHOP DIFFERENTLY

Shop ethically, buy secondhand and support locally made where possible.

Host a clothing or crockery swap with your friends. It's a great way to recycle, a lot of fun and you'll all come away with something 'new'. You might even want to do a coin donation to a local charity for every piece that's swapped.

RESPECT NATURE

Look after the planet and do your bit to live more sustainably. Start a vegetable garden or compost, get better at recycling, save more water, pick up rubbish.

HYGGE

DENMARK

WHAT IS HYGGE?

If you've been living under a rock for the past couple of years then you may not have heard of the delightful Danish cultural philosophy of hygge. For everyone else, we have been warmly surrounded by social media posts, blogs, articles and books dedicated to it. The concept has been commercialised throughout the world as lifestyle stores sell 'hygge blankets' and other hyggelig (the adjective form of the word) products. But hygge is not something you can buy. Hygge is very similar to the Dutch concept gezelligheid (*see* p.50), but hygge is usually associated more with winter whereas the Dutch concept is year-round.

While hygge might not be easy to translate, or pronounce (the closest you might get is 'hoo-guh' and not what you were saying in your head, like 'higgy'), it is thankfully something that is easy to get on board with. On the surface it's essentially all about fluffy warm socks, open fires, hot chocolate, candles and basically being cosy and comfortable. But it's also much more than that to Danes. It's more of a feeling than anything else – one of togetherness, warmth and contentedness. It's about sharing good times with your family, friends, loved ones and colleagues. Hygge is less about the fluffy warm socks and more about the fuzzy warm feeling you get when you cosy up with your loved one in front of an open fire while wearing your fluffy socks. It's sharing great food and conversation around your

dining table, or playing a board game, happy in the knowledge that you're indoors in the candlelight and warmth, while outdoors it is the middle of a Danish winter – dark and snowy.

Much like other Scandinavian countries, Denmark does very well on the World Happiness Report each year, coming in at number 1 in both 2013 and 2016 and at number 2 in 2020. Perhaps the cultural construct of hygge might explain why Danes are so happy all the time. Access to a good education, high-quality healthcare, a high standard of living and a stable government don't hurt either, but the idea of hygge means that Danish people recognise and value the small things in life and what's important.

WHERE DOES HYGGE ORIGINATE?

Surprisingly, the term hygge is not Danish at all but comes from the Norwegian language. The word is said to date back to the 16th century from an old Norwegian word 'hugga' that is thought to mean 'wellbeing' or something along the lines of 'to comfort' or 'to console'. The word hygge first appeared in Danish writing in the 18th century, and the Danes have embraced it ever since – hygge is now a fundamental part of the country's character. Its popularity has blossomed around the world, so much so that in 2016 it was shortlisted for the *Oxford English Dictionary*'s Word of the Year (it lost out to 'post-truth') and in 2017 it was officially added to the *Oxford English Dictionary* with the definition of: 'A quality of cosiness and comfortable conviviality that engenders a feeling of contentment or well-being (regarded as a defining characteristic of Danish culture).'

WHAT ARE THE HEALTH AND HAPPINESS BENEFITS?

IMPROVES SLEEP

Hygge is about creating a calm, relaxing and comfortable environment so if you add hygge into your nightly routine with a bit of self-care (see p.71), it can help relax you and send you off for a good night's sleep.

KEEPS US CONNECTED

Emotional connection and physical touch and intimacy play an important part in our mental and emotional wellbeing and can help with depression, reducing anxiety and boosting our endorphins. It boosts trust and strengthens our relationships.

HELPS US SWITCH OFF

After a busy day or week it can be hard to unwind and switch your mind off from the thousands of things buzzing around your brain. Incorporating hygge into your day can help you disconnect and reduce your stress levels. Making plans with a friend, or cooking up a big family feast is a good way to be in the moment and helps get your mind off other things. See p.71 for other ideas.

BOOST SEROTONIN LEVELS

Known as the 'happy hormone', serotonin is a chemical nerve that helps relay signals from one area of our brain to another and is associated with regulating mood and is thought to influence sleep, memory and sexual desire. An imbalance of serotonin is thought to lead to depression and anxiety, and research suggests that a lack of sunlight can contribute to this. There's not much sun around in a Danish winter, but hyggelig activities can boost your overall mood and make you feel good, which can increase your serotonin levels and make you feel happier.

WHERE IN DENMARK CAN I EXPERIENCE HYGGE?

While many Danes experience hygge at home by creating a dimly lit, warm and inviting atmosphere for hanging out in, you can also experience it out and about. Many bars, restaurants and cafes in Copenhagen exude a hyggelig environment. So as a visitor to Denmark you don't need to worry about waiting around for an invitation to someone's home. For a truly hyggelig experience, try visiting in winter and at Christmas time, in particular, when Denmark goes on hygge hyperdrive.

TIVOLI GARDENS

Opened in 1843, this historic garden is home to one of the oldest theme parks in the world. It attracts locals of all ages with its fantasyland vibe and dreamy collection of funfair rides, pavilions and delightful gardens. It's at its most hyggelig in the colder months when it turns into a winter wonderland with light shows and outdoor stalls selling mulled wine and traditional sweets.
See: tivoli.dk/en

JÆGERSBORGGADE

This is one of the liveliest streets in Copenhagen and is crammed full of boutiques, vintage stores, cafes and galleries. Take a friend and make a day of exploring, ducking in and out of shops and stopping for coffee breaks along the way.

COFFEE COLLECTIVE

Settle in with a book in a cosy spot and experience some hygge over a freshly brewed single-origin cup of coffee from the city's best micro-roastery. It's located on buzzing Jægersborggade.
See: coffeecollective.dk

BAKERIES AND TREATS

Nothing says warmth, comfort and hygge like the smell of baking bread and sweet treats wafting from a bakery. Copenhagen has plenty of places where you can fill up on freshly baked goodness but a few standouts include:

· Sankt Peders Bageri (pedersbageri.dk), the oldest bakery in the city dating back to the 17th century, has a cosy interior and is famous for its cinnamon rolls.
· Organic bakery Meyers Bageri (meyers.dk), is headed up by ex-Noma Chef Claus Meyer.
· La Glace (laglace.dk/en), the oldest pastry shop in Copenhagen, is full of old-world charm and delightful treats, such as walnut cake or the house specialty sportskage – a delectable cake of nougat, whipped cream, choux pastry and a macaron base.

HOW CAN I MAKE HYGGE PART OF MY DAILY LIFE AT HOME?

If all of this hygge business sounds tempting (and why wouldn't it?), there are some simple things you can do at home to bring hygge into your world. In terms of creating an atmosphere, focus on lighting (soft, candlelit, warm), texture (fluffy, cosy, soft – you're going for comfort over fashion here) and activities (fun, welcoming, calming, soothing, laidback).

A NIGHT WITH FRIENDS

Organise a catch-up with your friends, invite them over for a night of good food, chatting, laughing, playing board games, watching movies and just enjoying each other's company.

TIME TO YOURSELF

Sink into your favourite armchair, pop your feet up, wrap yourself in a blanket and spend hours absorbed in a good book or magazine. Keep your smartphone or device away!

HYGGE AT BEDTIME

Run yourself a bath with your favourite salts or oils, light a candle, pop on some music, lather yourself in lotion and then put on your comfiest clothes or PJs.

You might like to add a beautiful quilt to your bedding, sip a warm cup of herbal tea or a hot chocolate and make sure you turn off your devices an hour or so before bed – let hygge send you off on a peaceful night's sleep.

IKIGAI

JAPAN

WHAT IS IKIGAI?

What's your reason for getting out of bed in the morning? What motivates you? What's your passion and calling in life? Well, that could be your ikigai (pronounced 'ick-ee-guy'). Ikigai is composed of two words – iki, meaning life, and gai, describing value or worth. It's about finding the balanced mix of your passion, your satisfaction, your true self, your values and your calling. There is no direct translation in English, but ikigai loosely embodies the concept of finding happiness through knowing what your purpose in life is. But importantly it's not an individualistic ideal, rather it focuses on what the path for one person's happiness is and how they contribute to the greater society; everything is connected.

Often when we ask ourselves, 'what is the purpose of life?', we are thinking on a grandiose philosophical scale. But ikigai doesn't need to be a monumental, all-encompassing concept. It can relate to someone's work or family life, their hobbies or interests, travel, small personal goals and social identity. Better still, you don't have to be good at something for it to be your ikigai.

Ikigai can simply be enjoying the activity, the daily ritual – the thing that carries you through the day. It can also be about mastering a skill, if that's what you've identified is your ikigai. It is not the pursuit of money. While you might be someone who has been able to turn your ikigai into a

professional and financial success, it's not the essence of what ikigai is – just a fortunate by-product.

If you don't know what your ikigai is – don't worry. Some people are born knowing what they were put on this Earth to do and what their natural passion is, but most of us weren't. We need to work at identifying our ikigai and this can be a lifelong pursuit.

WHERE DOES IKIGAI ORIGINATE?

Ikigai has become somewhat of a wellness fad around the world in recent times but its birthplace is Japan. It's an age-old Japanese ideology. It's thought that the word ikigai actually dates way back to the Heian period in Japan (794– 1185 CE).

The concept of ikigai is often associated with the country's long life expectancy, particularly on the island of Okinawa, which is home to the highest ratio of centenarians in Japan. Some attribute this to the fact that many elderly Okinawans continue to actively work well past retirement age, by working on farms or fishing, for example. This gives them a purpose in life – ikigai. Others attribute their longevity to a healthy diet, active lifestyle and strong sense of community.

If you have heard about ikigai, read books on it or looked up the concept online, you would have most likely come across a Venn diagram supposedly representing ikigai. This is not the Japanese interpretation of ikigai, but is actually a reiteration of the Purpose Venn diagram. It might be helpful to have a look at it as a starting point, but it's handy to know this is not the origin of ikigai.

WHAT ARE THE HEALTH AND HAPPINESS BENEFITS?

The benefits of ikigai are pretty clear. If you don't have purpose, then this can have a negative effect on your mental and physical wellbeing. Studies have found that those who have ikigai are more likely to lead a happier and longer life. They have also shown that those with a purpose in life may be less likely to develop neurological illnesses, such as dementia, as well as other ailments, like stroke or cardiovascular disease.

Clinical psychologist and professor at Tokyo's Eiwa University, Akihiro Hasegawa is a leading authority on ikigai. When working with dementia patients at a psychiatric hospital, Hasegawa realised that those patients who had the will to live, had slower progressing dementia than other patients. This then motivated Hasegawa to research ikigai at graduate school.

If you're not one of the lucky ones who instantly know what their ikigai is, you will need to work at it a bit. Hasegawa teaches that it's important to understand that ikigai is a day-to-day concept, rather than thinking about your life as a whole. His studies and research papers show that there are a few things that are significant to having ikigai – strong family relationships, health, intellectual activeness and social behaviour all strongly influence a person's ikigai. Another important element according to Hasegawa is that a person feels they have control over their daily life and themselves. You are able to freely make choices and direct your life on your own path.

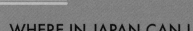

WHERE IN JAPAN CAN I EXPERIENCE IKIGAI?

Each individual is different and ikigai is a very personal thing. For one person, nature might be their ikigai; for another it might be painting and admiring art; for someone else it could be a passion for sport. Here are a few suggestions for places to visit in Japan that might just be the inspiration you need to identify your ikigai.

ART

Naoshima in the Seto Inland Sea is an incredibly scenic spot and is home to the Benesse Art Site (benesse-artsite.jp/en). The island is dotted with open-air sculptures and contemporary art galleries in striking buildings. It's most famous for world-renowned artist Yayoi Kusama's iconic yellow-and-black spotted pumpkin installation that sits at the end of the pier with the blue sea as its backdrop.

In the mountainous town of Hakone you can wander the hillside at its open-air art museum (hakone-oam.or.jp), admiring installations and sculptures by artists such as Miro and Henry Moore, before finding more inspiration among the hundreds of Picasso works in the Picasso Pavilion.

COOKING CLASSES

Conducted in a Japanese home, Uzuki (kyotouzuki.com) is a small-group cooking class in Kyoto where you can learn the delicate art of Japanese cuisine.

In Tokyo, learn how to make soba noodles from a master who has taught Michelin-star winning chefs at the popular cooking course, Tsukiji Soba Academy (soba.specialist.co.jp).

HIKING

The iconic Mt Fuji (3776m) is the country's highest and most famous mountain. It's a tough climb to the top, but a must-do for hiking enthusiasts. While many beginner hikers tackle the mountain, it's not without its challenges – the weather can turn quickly reducing visibility when the mist rolls in, altitude sickness is a serious risk, and the steep incline can be difficult on knees, especially when climbing down.

Kamikōchi is one of Japan's most well-known areas for outdoor pursuits, particularly hiking. There is a range of trails from pleasant signposted walks along the river to serious mountain peak climbs. The scenery is simply stunning – snow-covered craggy mountains are reflected in turquoise rivers, and in autumn (Sept to Nov) the region is ablaze with orange and red foliage.

For some serious self-reflection and inspiration, tackle the 88-Temple Walk on the island of Shikoku, which leads you along busy city highways to isolated mountain towns and onsen (hot-spring) villages. The entire walk is over 1400 kilometres (870 miles) long and takes anywhere from 40 to 60 days to complete, following in the footsteps of Kōbō Daishi, the monk who attained enlightenment and established the Shingon school of Buddhism in Japan.

MUSIC

If punk and rock music is your passion, Osaka is the place to be. The city has one of the best music scenes in the country and there are plenty of atmospheric live houses (live-music venues) where you can catch Japanese bands belting it out.

For classical music lovers, drop by Tokyo institution, Meikyoku Kissa Lion, a classical music cafe. Here you can be transported back in time as you listen to classical records through mammoth wooden speakers with incredible acoustics. If jazz is your genre of choice, pull up a chair at one of Tokyo's favourite jazz bars, The Pit Inn in lively Shinjuku, to hear a fantastic line-up of Japanese and international jazz musicians. See: pit-inn.com

SPORTS

Baseball is an obsession in Japan and no other city is quite so fanatical when it comes to their team as Osaka is with its Hanshin Tigers. If sport is what brings you joy, then don't miss the experience of a high-energy game here. Otherwise, watch the big boys go head-to-head during one of the season's wrestling tournaments at Japan's largest sumo stadium in Tokyo, Ryōgoku Kokugikan. The tournament is held in Tokyo in January, May and September.

HOW CAN I MAKE IKIGAI PART OF MY DAILY LIFE AT HOME?

Having something to enjoy, whether a daily ritual or a passion (your ikigai), may positively influence everything from your mental state to your immune system.

TALK TO OTHERS

Find out what motivates other people in your life and people from different backgrounds – friends, family, neighbours – and get ideas and inspiration from those in your circle.

KNOW YOURSELF

You need to get to know yourself, spend time with yourself and your thoughts. Take some time for some real self-reflection. Observe your thoughts and feelings honestly. Consider why you do things and what you spend your free time enjoying.

MAKE A LIST

Make a list of the things you enjoy doing, your core life values and things that you are good at. Examine the list and see what jumps out at you the most; what are you most drawn to?

TAKE TIME

Importantly, take time to decide. You don't have to determine what your ikigai is right here, right now. You might want to try being more creative, take a course or class, get fitter, be more social.

FIND AN INTEREST

Is there a creative pursuit that you've always wanted to follow? It could be food and cooking, gardening, art, reading or music. Now is the time.

Author and neuroscientist Ken Mogi refers to what he believes are the five pillars of ikigai in his book, *The Little Book of Ikigai* (2017). These five pillars help to build a framework when thinking about ikigai.

'**Pillar 1: Starting small.** Start by focusing on the small details. **Pillar 2: Releasing yourself.** You can do this by accepting who you are and being honest with yourself. It allows you to let go. **Pillar 3: Harmony and sustainability.** Recognise that you might need help and to rely on others. Everyone needs to connect with the people around us, this way you can learn from others and gain support. **Pillar 4: The joy of little things.** Learn to appreciate the small pleasures and what brings you joy. **Pillar 5: Being in the here and now.** Don't focus too far in the past or the future, be mindful in the moment and find your flow.'

Think about these five pillars in terms of your own life. How do they apply to you? How can you use these as a jumping off point for identifying your ikigai?

One of the leading authorities on ikigai was psychiatrist and author of *Ikigai-ni-tsuite (About Ikigai)*, Mieko Kamiya. Published in 1966, her book is still considered to be the authority on the topic of ikigai, and in it she explains that ikigai is what allows you to look forward to the future even if you're miserable right now. So chin up and start thinking about what might be your personal ikigai!

MERAKI
GREECE

WHAT IS MERAKI?

The Greeks are known for their passion. They pride themselves on their filoxenia (hospitality), their respect and honour for family, and their love for their country, all underpinned by a Greek concept called filotimo (loosely translated as 'love of honour'). They are lovers of music, dance, art, architecture and literature, and the country is revered for its artistic and cultural legacy. The Greeks have an enviable approach to life that is working to live, as opposed to living to work. They love life and know how to enjoy it. They live life to the fullest. When you're a visitor in Greece, you feel the warmth of their hospitality as you are invited to feast on home-cooked and often home-grown food.

What this encapsulates is one untranslatable Greek word – meraki. It means to do something with absolute devotion and passion, to put your heart and soul into something and to do it with love. While it usually relates to creative or artistic pursuits, meraki can be applied to any task. It might be singing, painting or dancing. It could be preparing and cooking a meal for your family and loved ones, it might be the thought and care you put into decorating a room or the effort put into a sporting match.

Meraki is about choosing to live a more meaningful life, to make the things you are doing count and have more of an impact. It means to put 100 per cent of yourself into the things that matter to you. In the words of Aristotle, 'Pleasure in the job puts perfection in the work'.

WHERE DOES MERAKI ORIGINATE?

It's not really a surprise to learn that meraki
(μεράκ)– a word whose meaning is tied up in
passion, devotion, total commitment – is borne
from the homeland of such magnificent feats
as the Acropolis, Knossos, *The Illiad* and the
marathon. This modern Greek word is said to be
derived from the Turkish word 'merak' to mean
labour of love or to do something with pleasure.

WHAT ARE THE HEALTH AND
HAPPINESS BENEFITS?

By devoting yourself to the task at hand, you are
being completely in the present moment. Total
concentration allows you to focus your efforts
and exclude any outside distractions, so that
your mind is clearer and wrapped up only in what
you are doing right here and now. You can't drift
off into worrying about the future or the past
when you are totally in the moment with a task
or project. It keeps your mind busy and on track.

We all know the feeling of satisfaction from
completing something that you have totally
thrown yourself at. It is far more rewarding
than if you do something half-heartedly. By
giving it your all, you're setting yourself up
for greater gains.

By doing something with meraki, you can also
find out what you really enjoy and what you're
truly good at.

WHERE IN GREECE CAN I EXPERIENCE MERAKI?

Anyone who has been to Greece has feasted their eyes on the incredible classical architecture and well-preserved historical landmark buildings that dominate the country. Visible from almost every vantage point in Athens is one of the Western world's most magnificent and important ancient sites, the World Heritage-listed Acropolis and the Parthenon. Or you might have visited one of the most significant archaeological sites in the world, the Minoan Palace at Knossos from the Bronze Age. Stand in the ruins of the Parthenon and Knossos and you can truly come to appreciate the phrase 'labour of love' and the meaning of the word meraki, albeit on a very grand scale.

Meraki doesn't refer to accomplishments only as monumental as the Acropolis! Watch locals in Greece congregate at cafes, socialising, laughing, dancing to traditional folk music and engaging in passionate and lively debate. The spirit of meraki is there.

In addition to standing in awe of its ancient architecture and generally observing the way Greeks go about their lives, there are many sources of inspiration – from art galleries and museums to theatre, music, opera and dance performances. You can stand in an art gallery and admire ancient Greek sculptures or bold contemporary art, where artists have devoted themselves to their work. You can watch actors display their passion in a gripping performance, listen to musicians reveal their heart and soul in their music, or witness a stirring, emotive opera performance by a tenor or soprano giving it everything he or she has got.

DANCE

There are many styles of dance throughout Greece and these vary region by region, and it's not all high-kicks, linked arms and Zorba. Some of the best places to see traditional folk dancing are as follows.

ATHENS AND EPIDAURUS FESTIVAL

Greece's foremost cultural festival is held at an ancient amphitheatre in Epidaurus in the Peloponnese and at the Odeon of Herodes Atticus in Athens. Here you can watch dance performances along with music and theatre during the summer months (June to Aug).
See: greekfestival.gr

DORA STRATOU DANCE THEATRE

This is one of the country's best places to see traditional folk dances in regional costumes, performed in an 860-seat open-air theatre in Athens.
See: grdance.org

MUSIC

ANOGIA, CRETE

If music's more your jam, the best place to be inspired and to witness artists with absolute devotion, soul and passion for their craft is in the town of Anogia on the island of Crete. This charming mountain town is the heartland of the instrument the lyra and birthplace of Crete's most famous singer, the late Nikos Xylouris. You can visit the small museum devoted to him here and might be lucky enough to catch local musicians jamming in the town's squares.

THE MEGARON

This is the leading performance venue in Athens and is particularly atmospheric in summer when you can see shows on the outdoor garden stage. It hosts an impressive line-up of performers, with everything from opera and theatre to dance and classical concerts. Don't miss the Music Library of Greece, where you can listen to a large choice of Greek music, ranging from traditional to contemporary works.
See: megaron.gr

OPERA

GREEK NATIONAL OPERA

Housed in a remarkable building at the Stavros Niarchos Foundation Cultural Center – designed by renowned architect, Renzo Piano – the Greek National Opera performs in its 1400-seat main auditorium. The season runs from November to June, and you can also catch performances as part of the Athens Festival in summer at the large amphitheatre, Odeon of Herodes Atticus (see p.84). See: nationalopera.gr

ART

To peek at the passion of some of Greece's best artists, head to these museums.

NATIONAL ARCHAEOLOGICAL MUSEUM

This is one of the leading sights in Athens and houses one of the finest collections of Greek antiquities in the world, some dating from the Neolithic era, in a beautiful Neoclassical building. Pieces on display include stunning pottery, incredible sculptures, impressive artefacts and elegant jewellery – a beautiful gold necklace that was recovered from a tomb in Spata, just east of Athens, is a real highlight, as is the gold death mask of Agamemnon, one of the most famous artefacts of the Greek Bronze Age. See: namuseum.gr

HERAKLION ARCHAEOLOGICAL MUSEUM

Dip into Crete's history at this excellent, state-of-the-art museum in a double-storey Greek Modernist building. This is one of Greece's most important museums as it houses artefacts that span 5500 years, from the Neolithic era to Roman times, including exhibits of Minoan masterpieces, such as the incredible Minoan snake goddess figurines. See: heraklionmuseum.gr

NATIONAL GALLERY

Athen's National Gallery collection includes over 20,000 artworks from the post-Byzantine era to the current day. The gallery has been closed since 2013 as it's being rebuilt and is expected to reopen in 2022. In the meantime, you can see a small selection of the works on display at the National Sculpture and Art Gallery. See: nationalgallery.gr

HOW CAN I MAKE MERAKI PART OF MY DAILY LIFE AT HOME?

If you love what you do and put soul into your activities and tasks, it is something that seeps into your everyday attitude, outlook and way of life.

For some of us, we might be lucky enough to already be living the meraki way of life, pouring ourselves into our creative passions. For others, this might not be true. We might find ourselves coasting along. We might be exhausted from work, kids, pets, grocery shopping and household duties, and we don't have the time to indulge in creative pursuits. But we can all live our lives a bit more meraki style if we choose to – it doesn't need to be a monumental undertaking.

When you take on a task, be it creative or otherwise, ask yourself, 'Am I giving this my 100 per cent? Can I put more effort and concentration into what I'm doing?' You might be working on a painting, or practising an instrument. It could be applying creativity and love to cooking your dinner or planting in your garden. Take a step back to reflect on your attitude to the task at hand. If you're not giving it all your passion and effort, why not? If it's not something you're enjoying then it will be tough to give your all. Try to work out what drives you creatively, what grabs your interest and what you really enjoy doing.

If you tend to get distracted easily, set aside a dedicated amount of time to work at your task and then have a break. Throw yourself into the work. Even if it's not your best work straightaway (and most likely it won't be), just stick with it and put in the time and effort. You'll find it easier to commit to it more and more each day and the more time you put in, the better the reward.

Start by thinking about what activities you are interested in and what brings you joy. Have you always wanted to try your hand at art? Well, now's the time to start. Find yourself a scenic spot (by a river, in the hills, at the beach), prop up an easel and start painting. Maybe you've always desired to become a dancer? Look online for local dance classes you can join.

You can also try adding meraki into your life by simply setting a beautiful dining table and inviting your friends or family over for a meal – lay out a lovely linen tablecloth and your best crockery, pop some fresh flowers on the table and light some candles. Really focus on the presentation and put a lot of love and effort into it to make the meal all that more special.

And with any creative activity, most importantly, avoid distractions by hiding your phone away and turning off the wi-fi so you're not tempted to jump online.

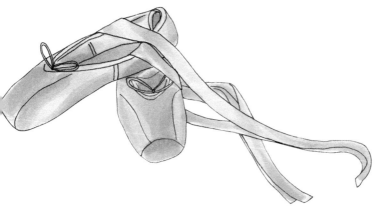

PURA VIDA

COSTA RICA

WHAT IS PURA VIDA?

It doesn't take long on a visit to Costa Rica until you start hearing the phrase pura vida everywhere – it's a significant concept in Costa Rican culture. It sits deep within the Costa Rican psyche and is a sense of love, belonging and community. Costa Rica consistently makes it near the top of the lists for one of the happiest places on Earth (coming in at 15th spot on the 2020 World Happiness Report) and this is in large part thanks to this phrase and philosophy. If you just learn one Spanish phrase when visiting Costa Rica, make it this one and you'll get far.

Pura vida means 'pure life' and it's a term that can be used as both a greeting and farewell for hello and goodbye; it can also be used to say 'I'm doing well', 'everything's cool', 'no worries', 'you're welcome' and 'that's life!' It's always a positive connotation. It won't take long until it's part of your everyday banter. While you're in the country, you'll see hostels, hotels, restaurants, bars and surf schools with the words 'pura vida' tacked on to their business name, and it will seep into your subconscious a little bit more each day.

Pura vida is not just a saying in Costa Rica but also a way of life. It reflects happiness, wellbeing and contentedness; it's something to be lived by. It's living the good life, enjoying a slow pace of life, being relaxed and laidback, spending quality time with loved ones and family, and appreciating and cherishing life's simple pleasures. When Costa Ricans utter the phrase 'pura vida', it is always accompanied by a wide, happy grin.

WHERE DOES PURA VIDA ORIGINATE?

No one can really define when the saying 'pura vida' was first used and where it came from, but it's been a part of Costa Rican culture for many years. One story has it that the phrase comes from a 1956 Mexican movie called *Pura Vida*, starring a comedian with a laidback, happy-go-lucky personality. Then the Costa Ricans took the phrase and ran with it.

It doesn't really matter what the story is, pura vida is now an intrinsic part of Costa Rica. It encompasses the true spirit and culture of the country.

WHAT ARE THE HEALTH AND HAPPINESS BENEFITS?

Costa Rica has consistently ranked as one of the top countries each year on the World Happiness Report by Gallup. It's also home to the Nicoya region, known as a Blue Zone region. A Blue Zone is a term given to a region in the world where the residents lead longer, healthier and happier lives, according to research carried out by National Geographic Fellow and bestselling author, Dan Buettner. Residents in Nicoya are said to live to be centenarians, thanks to a host of reasons – from eating a light dinner and enjoying physically active work to maintaining strong family and social networks and having a purpose in life.

Living the pura vida way seems to have an incredibly positive effect on people. In relation to many of its Central American neighbours, Costa Rica has relatively low poverty rates, a generally stable political situation and a higher standard of living.

Costa Ricans lead healthy and active lives by spending a large part of it outdoors. Getting

back to nature and staying active is all part of the 'pure life'. The country is blessed with lush rainforests that are home to abundant birdlife and wildlife, cascading waterfalls and lily-white sand beaches, making it the perfect spot for engaging with nature.

By living a slower and more relaxed pace of life, not being part of the rat race and not worrying over the small things, it results in lower stress levels and associated illnesses, which equates to a healthier society. Eating a healthy diet rich in tropical fruits, fresh seafood and nutritious beans, as most Costa Ricans do, and having plentiful sunshine and a beautiful environment doesn't hurt either!

WHERE IN COSTA RICA CAN I EXPERIENCE PURA VIDA?

Pura vida is everywhere in Costa Rica. It permeates every aspect of daily life. As a visitor, friendly locals will greet you wherever you go with a big smile and well wishes of pura vida.

The stunning Costa Rican nature and scenery makes it easy to let go, slow down and live in the moment, to feel the essence of pura vida. Take in the views of lush rainforests, palm tree-backed beaches and serene lapping waters. Leave your stress and worries behind you as you soak in volcanic hot springs, let waterfalls rain down on you, sink into a hammock with a good book or laze away the afternoon basking in the sun on a stretch of soft sand at the beach.

Pura vida is also about getting outdoors, staying active and healthy, and the country has no shortage of outdoor adventures to try. If you're

a bit of an adrenaline junkie, you can tackle the rapids white-water rafting. If you prefer your activity a little less extreme, there are plenty of opportunities to get on a yoga mat, head out on the waves surfing or stand-up paddleboarding, or strap on your hiking shoes.

For a quintessential pura vida experience, book yourself a stay at a small family finca (farm), such as at Albergue El Socorro (albergueelsocorrosarapiqui.com), outside of San Miguel in the Sarapiquí Valley. The region is dotted with farms and pastureland and is great for wildlife watching (monkeys, birds, sloths), hiking and white-water rafting. Albergue El Socorro is the perfect place to unwind, escape and take some time out from the bustle of everyday life to experience authentic Costa Rican rural life. You can discover nearby waterfalls, lend a hand on the farm and head off on rainforest hiking trails.

HOW CAN I MAKE PURA VIDA
PART OF MY DAILY LIFE AT HOME?

FOCUS ON THE IMPORTANT THINGS

Family, friends, nature, wildlife, having enough good food and drink.

TAKE TIME OUT

It's important to make time for relaxing and unwinding. It might be curling up with a book, lying on the couch to watch a movie, soaking in a bath, getting a massage, whatever makes you feel calm and relaxed.

SLOW DOWN

It's hard to avoid getting caught up in the fast-paced lifestyle that many of us lead. Try to slow things down and not be in a hurry all the time. Pura vida means not worrying about the clock so much.

BE IN THE MOMENT

Stop, look around, be present and be mindful. Don't get too caught up in what's happened in the past or what might happen in the future. Live in the present moment and connect with what's happening right now. Savour a beautiful view, really taste a home-cooked meal, listen to the sound of birdsong or kids playing in the street. Soak it all up.

STAY POSITIVE

Try not to get caught up in the irritating things that happen to everyone at some point in life. When things are not going the way you would like, try to stay calm and in a positive frame of mind – focus on the good things instead.

LESS IS MORE

Pura vida is about simplicity. It's not a competition of who can have the biggest TV, the best car or the mansion with a pool. It's not about the quantity of your possessions, but the quality. Less is more.

GET ACTIVE

Costa Ricans spend a lot of time outdoors in the sun getting a healthy dose of vitamin D, whether it's fishing and farming, surfing, hiking or swimming. So join a local sporting club, take up running or jump in the pool and thrash out some laps. By being active, you are releasing endorphins, which make you happier.

ROMANTICISM
ENGLAND

WHAT IS ROMANTICISM?

When you hear the word Romanticism, you might think of candlelit dinners, long walks on the beach and celebrating Valentine's Day. But despite the name, Romanticism is not actually linked to sentiments of love. It was an artistic and intellectual movement that started around the late 18th century in Europe, and flourished until the mid-19th century, spreading across the world.

The movement embraced ideals of nature, passion, imagination and emotion in art, music and literature. Writers, poets, artists and musicians of the Romantic period were disillusioned with the philosophy of the Age of Reason or the Enlightenment, and they intentionally shifted away from that more structured, cerebral approach to the arts. The Romantics challenged the notion that reason and order was the only acceptable way to view the world, arguing that emotions, respect for nature and sensitivity were equally as important. This was their creative driving force; artists were looking to provoke an emotional response from their audience with their art.

While the Romantic era and the Enlightenment shared the same idea of the individual perspective, Romanticism was more of an introspective approach, which focused more on the individual's imagination, emotions

and personal expression to explore the more spiritual side of humans and the beauty of nature. As the French poet Charles Baudelaire described it in 1846, 'Romanticism is precisely situated neither in choice of subject nor in exact truth, but in a way of feeling.'

Romanticism covered a broad variety of styles and subjects, from painting and sculpture to literature, architecture and music. The Romantic artists mainly worked with paint, and landscape painting was the leading genre. British painter J.M.W. Turner is considered to have been the leading artist for the Romantic landscape genre. He was inspired by a trip to Switzerland, with its stunning landscapes, beginning in him a fascination with nature which he expressed in his art.

Romantic-era painters such as Turner, John Constable, Francisco Goya, Eugène Delacroix and Antoine-Jean Gros closely observed nature – the landscape, animals, sea and sky – and often worked en plein air (in the outdoors). Certain artworks, including those depicting war and the French Revolution, portrayed not only the beauty of nature but also the power and destructibility. These works evoked feelings of horror, awe and respect in the paintings' audience, achieving the emotional response from the viewer that Romanticism was all about.

Poets such as William Blake, Samuel Taylor Coleridge and William Wordsworth started Romanticism in British literature with their sensitive works. The second generation followed on, with the likes of Percy Bysshe Shelley, Lord Byron and John Keats, while the incredible imagination of Mary Shelley's most famous work,

Frankenstein, is considered by some critics to have taken the idea of Romanticism to an entirely new level.

In America, poets Edgar Allan Poe and Walt Whitman were prominent in the Romantic period. During this time, poetry spoke of nature and the relationship between nature and humans, it expressed strong emotions and individuality.

The Romantic period in music started around 1830 and ended around 1900, with some of the most well-known composers, such as Ludwig van Beethoven, Richard Wagner, Franz Liszt and Pyotr Ilyich Tchaikovsky. Although Beethoven died just before the start of the Romantic period, he is considered to have pioneered Romanticism in music by breaking free of the formal restraint of classical music at the time and creating a new approach.

Musical compositions became more intense and passionate, more expressive and inventive, with dramatic operas, expanded orchestras, a larger range of pitch and virtuoso piano music being influenced by the art and literature of the time.

Romanticism was a movement of ideas and it created a monumental shift in the Western world.

WHERE DOES ROMANTICISM ORIGINATE?

There are many thoughts and ideas on where and when Romanticism first developed and it's tricky to accurately pinpoint the exact start of the movement. It's widely believed to have started in England and Germany before sweeping across the rest of Europe and into the US, and it's thought that the term first appeared in literary criticism around 1800. Others say that Friedrich Schlegel, the German poet, is credited as the first person to use the word romantic as a way to describe literature depicting emotions in an imaginative form.

Romanticism can be traced back to a number of events around the time of the mid-18th century, and some of the earliest examples seem to have been influenced by German folklore, such as the Brothers Grimm fairytales, and old English ballads. It was also largely influenced by nationalism and the French Revolution, and artists used their art as a way of dealing with the trauma and expressing their feelings in a way that hadn't been done before.

WHAT ARE THE HEALTH AND HAPPINESS BENEFITS?

By tapping into a Romanticism mindset, we open up our emotional awareness and our ability to express these emotions freely. The fundamental idea of Romanticism was to break free from restraints, to express oneself, to be in touch with your emotions and to think imaginatively and creatively.

As human beings our emotions are what drive most of us – anger, happiness, excitement, fear. If we bury our emotions it can have devastating and long-lasting effects on our mental and physical wellbeing. Whether it's creative expression through music, art, dance or poetry, or simply through having a conversation with a friend, we benefit from expressing our emotions as it helps us release that energy and it lets others know how we're feeling so they can be more understanding. Showing vulnerability helps develop deeper and more meaningful relationships.

Romanticism also laid emphasis on the importance of the individual and was quite revolutionary in its ideas – it encouraged people to use their own imagination, to break free from the past and to follow their own ideals, rather than the imposed rules and conventions. Artists were interested in the quest for liberty and denouncing certain social constructs, such as the exploitation of the poor and the slavery of women.

Nature also played a crucial part in Romanticism and artists portrayed a deep respect for it, from the sublime English countryside in the oil paintings of Turner and Constable to Wordsworth's love of nature evident in his poems. Romanticism can remind us just how powerful and important the natural world is and the affect it can have on us physically, mentally and spiritually.

WHERE IN ENGLAND CAN I EXPERIENCE ROMANTICISM?

Whether you want to head for the hills and step into the very landscapes that inspired Wordsworth, Blake, Turner and Constable or you'd prefer to view the artists' perspective in the artworks and poems themselves, England offers plenty of opportunities.

WORDSWORTH HOUSE AND GARDEN

Visit the birthplace and childhood home of the poet William Wordsworth in Cockermouth, Cumbria. It was here that he first learned his two loves – nature and literature – and where, as a child, he enjoyed roaming the countryside and reading from a collection of books in the home.
See: nationaltrust.org.uk/wordsworth-house-and-garden

GRASMERE

The delightful village of Grasmere, Cumbria, is a famous pilgrimage site for literary lovers and those interested in Romanticism. This is where you'll find Dove Cottage, the home of Wordsworth from 1799 to 1808, at the end of a lake and surrounded by rolling hills and woodlands.

COLERIDGE COTTAGE

Located in Nether Stowey in Somerset, this 17th-century cottage was the home of poet Samuel Taylor Coleridge for three years from 1797. During his short but pivotal time here he wrote some of his best known works, including *The Rime of the Ancient Mariner* and *Frost at Midnight*. Visitors can explore the house and stroll the garden to get an insight into where Coleridge's inspiration came from.
See: nationaltrust.org.uk/coleridge-cottage

TATE BRITAIN

Stand in awe of one of the Romantic masters of landscape painting at the Tate Britain gallery in London, which houses the largest collection of works by J.M.W. Turner.

WINCHESTER

Follow in the footsteps of John Keats – who spent time in Winchester in 1819 – on a ramble through the countryside that inspired him to pen one of his most famous works, *To Autumn*. On a visit here it's not hard to see why Keats was so taken with this charming town – Winchester is rich in history, with a glorious medieval cathedral and a picturesque river valley setting.

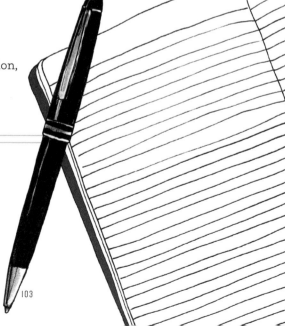

HOW CAN I MAKE ROMANTICISM PART OF MY DAILY LIFE AT HOME?

We can't all expect to look at a beautiful English country scene and then with a dab of a paintbrush or scribble of a pen turn out a masterpiece of art or poetry. But we can look at the ideals of Romanticism – nature, individual expression and emotional awareness, and apply them to our own life.

APPRECIATE THE BEAUTY AROUND YOU

The Romantics took time to see the beauty in things. Go for a walk in a forest or your local park. Find a spot to sit and take it all in. Look at its beauty but also try to reveal its power, its unpredictability. If you're lucky to get a blue-sky sunny day, look at the way the light hits and illuminates objects, leaves, treetops, grass, other people. If it's a grey, moody day, notice the way the rain might fall in droplets and land on leaves, what is the wind doing to the environment, is it destructive in its nature? Make observing nature a part of your daily life.

SPARK YOUR CREATIVE SIDE

We can all look to discover our own inner creativity, and who knows you might be the next Turner or Wordsworth! Enrol in a drawing class or grab some paint and a canvas and head outdoors for some plein air inspiration. Read a poetry book – there are some collections that give you a poem for every day of the year, so that you can read works by all different poets and from different time periods. Or try your hand at writing a poem yourself or pick up a new musical instrument. Try to keep in mind the emotional awareness and personal imagination aspects of Romanticism when you work.

GET IN TOUCH WITH YOUR EMOTIONS

Some of us wear our heart on our sleeve, while for others it's tough to let our emotions out. First, sit and think about how you're feeling, recognise your emotions. Are you angry, fearful, anxious, excited, filled with joy, nervous? Don't judge yourself, just be aware. Meditation can be a helpful tool for this. Find a quiet spot, get yourself into a comfortable sitting position on the floor, on a cushion or seated on a chair, and allow at least 10 minutes. Close your eyes and try to focus on how you feel but don't linger on any thoughts or feelings for too long – just recognise it and then let it go. This should help you get in touch with your emotions, as well as help calm your mind and body.

SHINRIN YOKU

JAPAN

WHAT IS SHINRIN YOKU?

The portmanteau for the Japanese words for forest (shinrin) and bath (yoku), shinrin yoku or 'forest bathing' is a nature therapy and simply refers to taking a break in nature and really basking, or 'bathing', in the atmosphere. The term 'forest bathing' can be somewhat misleading. It might conjure images of someone soaking in a warm bath plonked in the middle of a national park, or perhaps lowering yourself into a tub at home piled high with garden cuttings. The reality of the experience is much simpler, with far less cause for public humiliation or running the risk of poison ivy getting into some unwanted delicate areas.

This type of 'bathing' is seen as a way of self-healing by immersing yourself in nature and the outdoors, outside of your home or office, and away from your computer or smartphone screen. Forest bathing doesn't involve grabbing your walking sticks and climbing a mountain or other gruelling activities. Instead, it focuses on slowing things down, taking a break, meandering, breathing in fresh air and stopping to allow a sensory immersion of your external environment. The importance of the experience is putting yourself in the present moment, being consciously aware of your surroundings and of being in nature.

WHERE DOES SHINRIN YOKU ORIGINATE?

The concept was developed in Japan in the 1980s and the director of the Agriculture, Forestry and Fisheries Agency at the time, Tomohide Akiyama, coined the term shinrin yoku.

The high-stress work demand of the economic boom in corporate Japan in the 1980s was starting to take its toll on the health of businesspeople throughout the country. Karoshi (death by overwork) was becoming a serious health issue, with people dying from heart attacks and strokes.

The aim was to help people escape the excesses and stresses of the economic boom time by reconnecting with nature and thus, shinrin yoku was developed as the cornerstone of preventative medicine in an attempt to reduce medical costs in the country.

Today, forest bathing has not only become a popular health therapy in Japan, its popularity has also spread throughout the world.

WHAT ARE THE HEALTH AND HAPPINESS BENEFITS?

It is becoming more and more important in these modern, stressful, device-dominant times to disconnect from our busy daily lives and reconnect with nature. Most of us are spending a lot more time indoors surrounded by smart TVs, laptops, toxic appliances, and smartphones beeping and vibrating; all of these are constantly vying for our attention and causing 'technostress'. This can lead to a host of ailments from anxiety, headaches and depression to irritability and insomnia.

The first step to remedying this is simply getting out of the high-stress environment and into the outdoors, and there are plenty of reasons for doing so. Forest bathing is said to have a number of significant health benefits – by opening ourselves up to nature and our senses, we can start to reconnect, relax and slow down.

Research that was conducted at the time of the initial development of shinrin yoku showed the immense health benefits attributed to taking a walk in nature, taking time out and really slowing things down. Studies showed that such activity could reduce blood pressure, lower cortisol levels and improve concentration and memory, and a chemical released by trees and plants called phytoncides was found to boost the immune system. As more and more research and studies supported this theory, the Japanese government incorporated shinrin yoku into its national health program.

Dr Qing Li (*see* p.114) from Tokyo's Nippon Medical School is one of the leading experts on forest bathing and forest medicine. Dr Li's research has shown that those who walked in the woods had significantly lower blood pressure and increased levels of energy. It also found that forest therapy increased your natural killer cells, the ones that get rid of dead or dying cells – cancer-fighting cells – as trees give off phytoncides, which are natural oils of a tree or plant that protect them from bacteria and insects. A study conducted by Li showed that exposure to phytoncides had a number of benefits, ranging from better sleep and lower levels of stress hormones to an increase in these natural killer cells and a stronger immune system.

WHERE IN JAPAN CAN I EXPERIENCE SHINRIN YOKU?

It's no surprise Japan is the birthplace of shinrin yoku, considering that two-thirds of the country is covered in forest and it's home to over 30 national parks. On top of this, there are 64 forest therapy bases – forests that have been certified by a forest therapy expert as being appropriate for the activity and that contain at least two suitable walking paths. There are countless places to experience forest bathing in Japan. The following are some of my favourite spots.

AKASAWA NATURAL RECREATIONAL FOREST

Situated in Kiso, Nagano, this large forest is one of the first forest therapy bases and considered to be the birthplace of shinrin yoku. It's also one of the country's most beautiful forests and is home to 300-year-old Kiso hinoki (Japanese cypress) trees and features a number of walking trails.

YAKUSHIMA NATIONAL PARK

Located on Yakushima Island – a UNESCO World Heritage Site – this park is home to some of the world's oldest trees; the ancient yakusugi (Japanese cedar) is over 1000 years old. While the park is a place for serious hikers with its steep mountains and wild interior, there are spots of the forest just perfect for experiencing some forest bathing among moss-covered stones, babbling creeks and waterfalls. Parts of the forest are said to have inspired scenes in Hayao Miyazaki's much-loved animation film, *Princess Mononoke*.

CHUBU-SANGAKU NATIONAL PARK

This park covers a large part of the Northern Japan Alps and has some of the country's most impressive mountain peaks and some incredible dramatic scenery, with ancient looming beech and cedar trees, crystal-clear creeks and steaming onsen (hot springs).

MT TAKAO

Takao-san can be visited easily on a daytrip from Tokyo (only an hour west from Tokyo's Shinjunku train station on the Keio line) and is a hugely popular hiking spot – try to avoid weekends when it can get really busy. Hiking trail number 1 is the most popular and has a paved walking track, but for a more back-to-nature feel, take the very pleasant and less-visited trail number 6.

HOW CAN I MAKE SHINRIN YOKU PART OF MY DAILY LIFE AT HOME?

You don't need to visit Japan's mighty national parks and mountains to have a go at shinrin yoku, as the beauty of this nature therapy is that it can be done almost anywhere.

Even if you don't live near a forest or national park, you can take yourself to a local city park or sit in your garden. All you need is a plant- or tree-filled area outdoors where you can grab a slice of time to walk or sit in a relaxed way. Remember that it's not about rigorous exercising or a strenuous activity. The focus is on connecting with the natural environment.

Ideally you will set aside at least a couple of hours for your forest bathing session, but if you are time-poor even a quick 20- or 30-minute break will deliver its benefits.

Here are some basic steps to consider when setting off for a spot of shinrin yoku.

BE OBSERVANT

Be aware of your surroundings and take it all in. Tune into your senses. Notice the sounds of people, animals, the wind. Look at the detail of different leaves, the bark of a tree. Run your fingers over them. What birds can you hear? Can you smell the scent of the forest, the flowers, the leaves, the soil? Shinrin yoku is an intentionally slow exercise, carried out at a snail's pace with the emphasis on this mental awareness rather than the physical activity.

GO SLOW

When you walk, do it slowly and steadily at a leisurely wandering pace so that you can observe your environment. Stay focused on this pace, don't rush yourself and try not to become distracted.

TAKE A MOMENT

Make some time to find a spot to just sit. Maybe it's by a pond in a park, or under a shady tree in your backyard. Try to allow at least 20 minutes or so for this as a quiet meditative activity. Stay present and aware but let thoughts and noise drift over you. If possible, lie down and look up at the sky, study the clouds. If you work in an office, head outside for a short break, take off your shoes and just walk around on the grass. Taking a moment doesn't need to be big; small things can help you get in touch with the benefits of being in nature.

If you don't like the idea of going it alone on your forest bathing session and you're looking for some guidance, there are plenty of forest bathing organisations around the world that offer guided experiences for individuals or groups. Look them up in your local area. According to the Association of Nature and Forest Therapy (natureandforesttherapy.org), there are now about 1500 accredited forest-bathing guides worldwide.

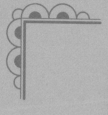

INTERVIEW

Dr Qing Li

From the Nippon Medical School in Tokyo, president and founding member of the Japanese Society of Forest Therapy and author of *Forest Bathing: How Trees Can Help You Find Health and Happiness* (2018) and *The Art and Science of Forest Bathing* (2018).

HOW DO YOU DEFINE SHINRIN YOKU?

Shinrin yoku is like a bridge. By opening our senses, it bridges the gap between us and the natural world.

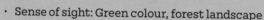

People can enjoy shinrin yoku through the five senses:

- Sense of sight: Green colour, forest landscape
- Sense of smell: Special good smells, fragrance
- Sense of hearing: Forest sounds, birdsong
- Sense of touch: Touching trees, putting your whole body in the forest atmosphere
- Sense of taste: Eating foods from a forest, tasting the fresh air in a forest.

WHAT DO YOU CONSIDER TO BE THE MAIN HEALTH AND WELLBEING BENEFITS OF SHINRIN YOKU?

1. Reduced blood pressure and stress – it can reduce the heart rate and stress hormones such as cortisol, adrenaline and noradrenaline, which may have a preventative effect on cardiovascular disease.
2. May have a preventative effect on cancers – it increases the number of natural killer cells and the intracellular levels of anti-cancer proteins. Natural killer cells are immune cells and play an important role in defense against bacteria, viruses and tumours.
3. Improved sleep and mood – it can have a preventative effect on sleep disorders and also reduce the symptoms of anxiety, depression, anger, fatigue and confusion.

WHAT IS THE MINIMUM LENGTH A SHINRIN YOKU SESSION SHOULD LAST TO REAP THE BENEFITS FROM IT?

If you want to boost your immunity (natural killer activity), a three-day/two-night trip is recommended, where you can hike and camp to really immerse yourself in nature for a longer period of time.

If you just want to relax and relieve stress, a daytrip to a forested park near your home would be recommended.

SISU

FINLAND

WHAT IS SISU?

We've all had to go through trying times in our lives, some more than others. As humans we face challenges and hardships all the time, but somehow we get through them. This perseverance is at the heart of the Finnish concept of sisu (pronounced see-soo). Facing adversity, displaying perseverance in a challenging time and mustering your inner strength, this is sisu. It's what you dig deep for when you come up against a rough patch or a difficult task. It's the mental strength that sees you through something until the end. You might consider it backbone, to have guts, integrity, determination or spirit. In essence, sisu is fortitude. It's a kind of psychological power and has been compared to the English phrase 'stiff upper lip' and the Japanese 'ganbaru' with similar sentiments.

Sisu doesn't only apply to monumental challenges or life-changing moments, such as the death of a loved one, a devastating accident or attempting to climb a mountain. It can, of course, relate to these events, but it's also something that can be applied to any area of life, whether it's problem solving at work, dealing with tough relationship issues or learning a musical instrument.

Finland was voted the happiest country in the world in 2020 in Gallup's World Happiness Report, and this is something Finns attribute in part to their cultural concept of sisu, ingrained in them from a young age. By facing challenges and struggles head on, it enables people to feel confident, resilient and, ultimately, happier.

WHERE DOES SISU ORIGINATE?

Use of the word sisu dates as far back as the 1500s and it is said to originate from a root word meaning inner, guts or the intestines.

Finns often cite the hardships of the country's history – wars and famine – and the brutally harsh, cold weather, as an explanation for how sisu became so ingrained in the Finnish people's character and identity.

WHAT ARE THE HEALTH AND HAPPINESS BENEFITS?

In her book *Finding Sisu*, Canadian-born and Helsinki-based author Katja Pantzar (*see* p.122) writes about some of the different ways Finns incorporate sisu into their lives. One of these activities is ice swimming in winter. Not the first thing that comes to mind when thinking of what might put a smile on someone's face, yet Katja tells the story of how she started winter swimming with some Finnish friends and after the initial shock, she was able to keep at it and build up sisu; by the end of the season she was not just persevering through it but actually enjoying it and relying on it. When winter swimming, Katja experienced a rush of endorphins and it helped improve her mood so much that she writes about replacing an evening drink to relieve stress with a quick icy dip. By displaying sisu, she in effect became happier.

No one is suggesting that to be happy and healthy you have to slide into your swimming gear and rush out to the sea in near-freezing temperatures – unless that's your thing. But there are some health benefits to be had from following in the Finns footsteps and displaying sisu.

GIVES A SENSE OF CONFIDENCE

Sticking with a problem or challenge when you just want to give up, and then suddenly managing to overcome it gives you a real confidence boost and increased self-esteem. You are more likely to then take some risks and try new things. You can find happiness in the control you have over your life and tricky situations that arise.

HELPS ACHIEVE GOALS

Practise makes perfect. Anyone who had to learn a musical instrument as a child will know this all too well. By not giving up and pushing yourself, you give yourself a better chance of becoming better at something. Perhaps it's creative writing or swimming, or learning how to overcome a fear of heights. Whatever it is, sisu can help you achieve your goals.

BUILDS RESILIENCE

Coping with stress is an important skill to have. Sisu is about resilience and overcoming adversity, which can help us cope with whatever challenges we might face, from dealing with grief to losing your job or tackling a big work project to deciding to swim the English Channel. Resilience also helps reduce stress, depression and anxiety and improve overall wellbeing.

For all the positives of sisu, it can actually have some negative sides if it's not approached in the right way. By persevering with things with a 'fight or die' attitude, it can lead to burnout and exhaustion. We can't all face our challenges alone and without support, either. The concept of sisu can suggest that asking for help is a sign of weakness, but we all need to rely on friends and family and a support network in difficult times to help get us through – whether we have sisu or not.

HOW CAN I MAKE SISU PART OF MY DAILY LIFE AT HOME?

CHALLENGE YOURSELF

The Finnish are known for their love of nature and deep connection to being outdoors. Take their lead and tackle the great outdoors yourself. Push yourself to do something new – if you're not a hiker, take up hiking. If you're not good on a bike, start mountain biking. Take some risks and challenge yourself. And if you start off with 1 kilometre, push it to 2 kilometres the next time and use sisu to help you achieve your goals.

RESILIENCE TRAINING

You can train yourself in how to become more resilient, and there are actually organisations that run courses if you're really keen. One easy way to do this yourself at home is through the practice of mindfulness and meditation. This allows your brain to take a break, to calm down and think more clearly in times of stress.

TAKE TIME TO RELAX

To avoid the sisu burnout effect, try to add some relaxation into your daily routine. The Finns have their sauna ritual but if you don't have access to a sauna at the gym or local pool, recreate the experience in your own bathroom as best you can. Run a hot bath, light a candle, add some relaxing bath salts, grab your book and settle in.

BELIEVE IN YOURSELF

It might sound a little cliché, but it's true. Most important of all is to have courage, trust yourself and believe in your own abilities. Be confident and brave. You probably have bucketloads of sisu already – you just didn't know it.

INTERVIEW
Katja Pantzar

Helsinki-based author of *Finding Sisu: In Search of Courage, Strength and Happiness the Finnish Way* (2018).

WHAT DOES THE CONCEPT OF SISU MEAN TO YOU PERSONALLY? HOW WOULD YOU BEST DESCRIBE IT TO SOMEONE WHO HAS NEVER HEARD OF IT?

Sisu is a Finnish word that refers to a special quality of fortitude and resilience, especially in the face of great challenges. Not only does it mean tackling life's obstacles headfirst – even when they can seem impossible – but a good sense of sisu can set you up for trying daring physical activities, such as cold water or winter swimming that can boost your wellbeing.

WHAT ARE SOME EXAMPLES OF THE WAYS YOU HAVE DEMONSTRATED SISU IN YOUR LIFE?

Swimming in the Baltic Sea just about every day is one way that I practice daily sisu. (I just returned from a dip in the sea, which is about 10°C/50°F in spring.)

The great surprise for many who try cold-water swimming or winter swimming for the first time is the post-dip feeling of euphoria. Swimmers feel energised and exuberant, as the immersion in cold water releases the so-called happy hormones. These include endorphins, the body's natural painkillers, serotonin (widely thought to maintain mood balance), dopamine (the neurotransmitter that helps control the brain's reward and pleasure centres and also helps to regulate movement and emotional response), and oxytocin (also known as the love hormone).

The cold water also enhances blood circulation, burns calories, and the immune system gets a boost – according to research. Many devotees follow up their icy dip with a sauna, the quintessential Finnish steam bath, where bathers (men and women sauna separately) sit without swimsuits – another test of getting comfortable with a little discomfort – sisu for the uninitiated.

WHAT INSPIRED YOU TO WRITE A BOOK ABOUT SISU?

I saw so many examples of sisu, or daily fortitude, in action that helped people with their wellbeing and I wanted to share these with readers. And many of the examples from the Nordic lifestyle that I highlight in my book are quite simple and sensible and can be incorporated into daily life, whether it's spending more time in nature, cycling as a form of transport year-round, or trying out cold-water swimming for a natural energy boost.

DO YOU THINK SISU CAN BE USED BY ANYONE OR IS IT INHERENTLY A FINNISH THING?

I definitely think that a sisu approach to life can be adopted by anyone, anywhere.

SLOW FOOD

ITALY

WHAT IS SLOW FOOD?

We're all very familiar, too familiar, with what fast food is, but you mightn't be aware that there is also Slow Food – the antithesis of fast food. Slow Food advocates that we need to take a step back and examine our approach to how we eat and how we purchase food. It encourages people to buy locally and focus on supporting sustainable food practices, to enjoy the simple pleasures of food, to eat unhurriedly, and that eating slowly and locally leads to a healthier diet.

In our fast-paced lives, many people barely have the time to sit down for lunch or to prepare healthy, nourishing meals – let alone think about the food source, how it's produced and who produced it. There is generally a large disconnect between the origin of our food and what we see on our plate. Western grab-and-go attitudes to food are being fuelled by long working hours and busy lives dealing with family commitments and domestic duties – not to mention the hours we dedicate to social media and being glued to our screens. Take-away coffees, ready microwave meals, frozen processed foods, a quick dash to the local cafe for a sandwich to wolf down, drive-through take-away for dinner or delivered to your door thanks to food delivery services ... this approach to food might sound

familiar to a lot of people. And for many it's done out of necessity due to a lack of time, working long hours, rushing home late and being utterly exhausted. It can also come down to budget restraints, where fast food is seen as the cheaper option when compared to buying fresh, healthy produce to cook at home.

Enter the Slow Food Movement. This global organisation looks to challenge our fast food daily eating habits. Founded back in 1989 its aim is to 'prevent the disappearance of local food cultures and traditions, counteract the rise of fast life and combat people's dwindling interest in the food they eat, where it comes from and how our food choices affect the world around us' (slowfood.com/about-us).

The Slow Food Movement has grown substantially since its beginnings and now includes over 100,000 members from over 160 countries. All of these people work to the movement's manifesto of 'good, clean and fair food', that is food that is healthy and packed with flavour, food production that is not harmful to the environment, and that ensures producers are paid well and prices are accessible for most consumers.

WHERE DOES SLOW FOOD ORIGINATE?

Writer Carlo Petrini and a group of other Italian journalists from the town of Bra in Piedmont started the Slow Food Movement in 1989. McDonald's was just beginning to make its mark in Italy and the group was concerned about fast-food outlets threatening the country's strong gastronomic culture and history. Their aim was to defend regional traditions, good food and pleasure over speed and convenience with a sustainable approach.

The Slow Food Movement is involved in a number of projects globally to raise awareness of the benefits of Slow Food. In 2004, Petrini set up a gastronomy university in the town of Pollenza, not far from Bra, and the Slow Food Movement also hosts a biennial food festival in the Piedmont city of Turin. They have also developed an international catalogue of 'forgotten food products' or those in danger of extinction in the Ark of Taste project, which hopes to encourage people to seek out these foods, to have an interest in them and to keep cultivation of them alive. In order to be included in the catalogue, the foods must be of cultural or historical importance to a specific region.

WHAT ARE THE HEALTH AND HAPPINESS BENEFITS?

PROMOTES SUSTAINABILITY AND SUPPORTS LOCAL BUSINESSES

By choosing to adopt the Slow Food philosophy people purchase more locally grown produce, which has a host of benefits – from supporting local farmers and producers and boosting the local economy to reducing carbon emissions and food miles. By helping the local community, you're doing good and that boosts your mood and overall wellbeing. Pat on the back for you!

LEADS TO A HEALTHIER DIET

Becoming more educated on where your food comes from and how it's grown means you're less likely to choose processed food and more likely to eat a healthier diet of fresh fruit and vegetables. You might also become more inclined to eat healthier foods – free from hormones, chemicals, pesticides and preservatives. It also encourages eating food that is in season, where you get better quality and the food is more nutritious.

HELPS THE ENVIRONMENT

When you choose to follow a Slow Food ethos, you not only help yourself but also the environment.

Slow Food helps to reduce food miles and carbon emissions by cutting down on food being shipped around the world, it also cuts down on food waste and means less disposable plastic packaging. You tend to buy only what you need.

IMPROVES OVERALL HEALTH

By taking a Slow Food approach, you learn not to rush your meals and instead to take time out to savour the taste and relax. Also by not rushing food down you will know when you are full and when to stop eating, which can help with maintaining a healthy weight.. Slowing down also helps to reduce stress levels and gives you the opportunity to be in the present.

TASTES BETTER

It's simple. If you have bought fresh produce from your local farmers' market, you'll know that it just simply tastes better than what's on offer at a large supermarket. You don't even need to taste it; you can see it in the bright red plump tomatoes or in the sheen on a homegrown zucchini or the lush green leaves of a bunch of kale.

WHERE IN ITALY CAN I EXPERIENCE SLOW FOOD?

The first logical stop is the home of the Slow Food Movement – the Piedmont region, where you can roam the vineyards, hunt in the woods for truffles, shop at family run grocers and artisan food stores, and indulge in gelato and delectable chocolate.

PIEDMONT

For the ultimate selection of fine local food, try to time your visit for the biennial Salone del Gusto and Terre Madre (terramadresalonedelgusto.com/en) food expo that runs over five days in October in the city of Turin, with plenty of opportunities to chat with producers, sample goods and be part of workshops.

At Eataly in Lingotto (eataly.net/it_en/stores/turin-lingotto), you can stock up on a staggering selection of food and drink, from freshly baked bread and tempting Piedmontese beef to hulking wheels of cheese and homemade pasta at this Slow Food emporium in a converted factory.

Another fantastic place to shop is the family-run Latteria Bera in Turin, around since the late '50s, where the old-fashioned shopfront beckons with mouthwatering displays of cheese, wine, chocolate, biscotti and olive oils.

SARDINIA

If you want to experience true Slow Food, Sardinia is the place. Seek out organic grocers, feast on freshly caught seafood, and farm hop your way around the island for salami, meaty olives, honey, cheese and artichokes.

TUSCANY

Fertile Tuscany is a foodie hotspot and firm fixture on any gourmand's Italy tour. The region revolves around good food and drink with an emphasis on local seasonal produce.

POSITANO

The Slow Food Movement gave rise to a Slow City initiative and Positano is one of those towns in Italy which has been awarded the status. To be certified as a Slow City, a town must meet certain criteria, including having fewer than 50,000 residents, no fast-food outlets, prohibit the use of GMOs in agriculture, and include restaurants that serve traditional cuisine from local ingredients.

HOW CAN I MAKE SLOW FOOD PART OF MY DAILY LIFE AT HOME?

While the Slow Food Movement has millions of followers around the world, it also has its fair share of critics. One of the main criticisms is that it is elitist and only accessible to those with a decent income to afford it. And there is some truth to this – not everyone can afford to buy organic produce or meat – but adopting a Slow Food mindset doesn't mean having to go organic. It's about doing what you can within your parameters.

If your budget doesn't stretch to organic food, try to support your local farmers' market or grocer, instead of large supermarket chains, and get in the habit of only buying what you need. Local independent produce markets and grocery stores tend to stock more locally grown produce with comparable prices to supermarkets. Or you could grow your own food (*see* p.131). And by not wasting food, you are also not throwing money out in the garbage along with it.

BUY LOCAL

Shop at farmers' markets or local produce stores if you can. Don't be afraid to ask questions – Where does the produce come from? What is the farmer's relationship with the supplier? Are they sustainable and ethical? Find out what's in season as this produce is of course fresher and often cheaper too, as it hasn't been imported or stored for long periods of time.

ENJOY BREAKFAST

Start your day off with a slow breakfast – don't skip it or rush it. Set out the table with muesli, toast, eggs, coffee and juice. Turn on the radio or sit outside, leave your phone elsewhere. Concentrate on tasting the food, think about what's in it and savour it.

GROW YOUR OWN

Start your own vegetable and herb garden. It doesn't need to be a big undertaking – you can easily grow herbs and some vegetables such as potatoes and tomatoes in pots on a balcony. If you don't know how to start, head to your local garden centre to get advice or go for a walk in your neighbourhood and ask local gardeners about what grows well in your area. Remember that you'll need a decent potting mix for pots or a good mix of topsoil, compost, mulch and straw for garden beds.

(You can build your own raised beds or buy pre-made ones to save your back from bending down all the time to ground level.) It's important to position your vegetable garden in a spot where it will receive at least six full hours of sun for most veggies to thrive. You might like to plant fruit trees too, if you have the space. If you live in an apartment, you can grow your own herbs in pots.

COOK FOR YOURSELF

If you're someone who indulges in a lot of fast food, set a goal to cook all your meals for one week. Dust off a cookbook or download some recipes to get you started, or ask friends and family to share some with you. If you can already cook, try something new like making your own pasta or bread from scratch. You might even join a local cooking class to learn the basics or to make a particular sort of cuisine. Check labels to see where products are made and opt for locally produced ones.

EAT LOCALLY

When eating out, choose local restaurants over big chains or fast-food outlets, if you have the means to do so. You might even want to ask wait staff where the food is sourced from, so that you learn about your local suppliers, and find out what grows in your region.

TAI CHI

CHINA

WHAT IS TAI CHI?

Tai chi, Taijiquan in Chinese, is a form of martial arts but not the type you might usually visualise. Swapping vigorous kicking, punching and body contact for slow, rhythmic, gentle movements, tai chi is still a self-defence practice but it's more of a mind and body exercise that combines aspects of martial arts, meditation and ancient Chinese medicine. It focuses on cultivating qì (energy) in slow, deliberate movements, and is often compared with being closer to yoga than karate or kung-fu. Tai chi is closely linked to Taoist philosophy (*see* p.135), an ancient belief system from China, and at its most basic it is the aim of achieving a state of harmony of yin and yang.

Tai chi is a great exercise as it's safe and gentle for most age groups and is a popular form of exercise among the elderly in China. While there are many different styles of tai chi, they all use slow, fluid, graceful choreographed movements that flow from one gently into the next in a sort of dance-like sequence. So whether you're looking to get some physical exercise, relax the mind and body, learn a martial art or work on your breathing technique, tai chi is a perfect all-rounder.

The major styles of tai chi include Chen, Yang, Wu and Sun.

CHEN STYLE

The Chen style is the oldest style of tai chi from which all other styles are derived. It was created around the 17th century by retired Ming Dynasty army general, Chen Wangting, who was influenced by fighting techniques handed down through his family from his ancestors in the Chen Village. This style involves slow, deliberate movements alternated with more vigorous, quick and forceful strikes, therefore it is more in line with typical martial arts. It provides a solid cardio workout and is physically demanding.

YANG STYLE

Created by Yang Lu-chan in the early 19th century in China's Hebei province and developed from the Chen style, this is the most popular of the tai chi forms and the most widely practiced around the world. In its simplest form, the Yang style involves 24 movements but can be up to 108 in total. It's a somewhat physically challenging style as it requires you to keep a wider stance with bent knees for a lot of the time. This style of tai chi helps to improve flexibility by using large, exaggerated movements, and the gentle flowing sequences make it perfect for pretty much anyone to be able to practice it.

WU STYLE

This is the second most popular style practiced after Yang and was founded by Wu Chuan-yu who trained under the founder of the Yang style, Yang Lu-chan. This style differs from the others in that rather being centred and upright the emphasis is on extending the body by leaning forward and backwards. It also uses a smaller stance.

SUN STYLE

Developed at the start of the 20th century by Sun Lu-tang who was an expert in Xingyiquan and Baguazhang – two other internal martial arts – this is the newest of the major styles of tai chi. It uses higher upright stances with short, compact movements and open–close hand gestures. Movements are natural, gentle and simple, making it ideal for beginners, elderly people and anyone looking for a low-impact exercise. It's also a great choice for physical therapy and healing.

WHERE DOES TAI CHI ORIGINATE?

The precise origins of tai chi are largely unknown but there are several legends that claim to tell the story of its beginning. Some historians credit Chen Village as the birthplace of tai chi with the Chen style. Though according to popular folklore, the legendary Taoist monk Zhang Sanfeng from the mountains in Wudang Shan in north-west China, was the one who first created tai chi. It's believed that he was searching for a softer form of martial art when he witnessed a vicious battle between a crane and a snake one day. The snake used gentle flowing movements to avoid the attacks coming from the huge crane, which resulted in the crane eventually becoming exhausted and flying away. It's believed this was Zhang Sanfeng's inspiration for the tai chi sequences of movement he developed shortly after.

Tai chi also has an important connection to Taoism, a Chinese belief system with a history of over 2000 years. Taoism is about the balancing act of the two opposites, yin and yang, and Taoists believe that this push and pull from the opposites also happens in our bodies, much like in the universe, and that we must work to create harmony. Tai chi aims to move energy through our body to relieve areas of blockage and to balance the yin and yang.

WHAT ARE THE HEALTH AND HAPPINESS BENEFITS?

When it comes to the health benefits of tai chi, there are plenty of contradicting study results, and differing scientific and medical opinions. Proponents of tai chi believe that the practice can have a wide range of health and wellbeing effects, from delaying aging and strengthening muscles to reducing the risk of falls and boosting the immune system.

IMPROVES BALANCE AND STRENGTH

While tai chi is a low-impact and usually slow form of exercise, the body is in continuous motion and it is suggested that these movements can result in strengthening the arm and leg muscles, along with the core. This can help with balance and also to protect the joints.

STRENGTHENS THE IMMUNE SYSTEM

Studies undertaken by researchers at UCLA in 2003 suggest that tai chi, with its combination of physical movement and meditation techniques, can help to strengthen the immune system. It's thought that tai chi settles the nervous system, which can otherwise interfere with how strong the immune system is. This can lead to lower rates of illness and a decrease in issues with inflammation in the body.

REDUCES FALLS AND INJURIES

As tai chi is thought to help with balance and muscle strength, it also appears that it can help reduce the amount of falls and injuries, particularly among elderly people.

CALMS THE MIND

By using a combination of breathing techniques and slow, gentle movements, tai chi can quieten the mind and reduce symptoms of anxiety, stress or depression.

IMPROVES THE CARDIOVASCULAR SYSTEM

Tai chi helps the cardiovascular system by increasing blood flow through continuous movements and by increasing the amount of oxygen getting into the body through deep breathing. This is important for maintaining health and boosting the immune system.

WHERE IN CHINA CAN I EXPERIENCE TAI CHI?

Tai chi has been practiced for thousands of years in China and if you visit the country you will see many city parks and public spaces where groups of people gather to do tai chi together, usually early in the morning.

WUDANG SHAN

This mountain range in China's Hubei province is considered by many to be the birthplace of tai chi, so there is no better place to try your hand (and arms, and legs) at it. Wudang Daoist Traditional Kungfu Academy is the premier school to give it a go. There are options for courses from a few days up to one year if you're really keen!
See:
wudangwushu.com

TEMPLE OF HEAVEN, BEIJING

Spread over 267 hectares (659 acres), this park is home to what was once the most important temple in the city. The park has been open to the public since 1918 but before that was the private domain of the emperor. You can see groups of locals performing tai chi here. If you're brave enough, jump in and join them.

THE BUND, SHANGHAI

Shanghai's riverside promenade, The Bund, with its imposing Art Deco buildings, attracts early morning locals practising their tai chi moves to the backdrop of the river traffic and the retro Oriental Pearl TV Tower across the river in the Pudong district.

HOW CAN I MAKE TAI CHI PART OF MY DAILY LIFE AT HOME?

The first thing to consider is what style of tai chi is going to be right for you.

1. Are you a beginner or do you have some experience with tai chi or other martial arts?
2. Are you fit and healthy or do you need to ease into the practice?
3. Are you older or recovering from an illness or injury, particularly back or knee problems?
4. Do you want something low impact or would you prefer a more physically demanding style?
5. Are you interested in the martial arts aspect of tai chi or simply as a form of exercise?

Yang and Wu styles are good for beginners as they are easier to learn. As these styles are the most popular forms of tai chi, you shouldn't have a problem finding a local school offering classes, too.

If you're looking for something restorative or healing, try the Yang or Sun styles. The Yang and Sun styles involve upright stances, which don't place too much stress on the joints. If you want a more fast-paced cardio workout, Chen is your go-to.

Though it originates in China, tai chi has gained popularity across the world and it's not too difficult to find classes in most cities. Check your local area for martial arts schools offering guided tai chi classes. If you don't have any luck, head online to learn the basics, though it is recommended to have a guided class first if you're a beginner.

Once you have the basic movements, you can easily practise alone wherever you feel most comfortable. If you're not ready to put yourself in the public spotlight in your local park, try out some moves in your backyard instead. Or if you live in an apartment, why not entertain your neighbours on the balcony? If you're really not much of an exhibitionist you can simply try it indoors. You don't need much space at all, there's no equipment needed either. Just go at your own pace and enjoy the soft, gentle movements.

UBUNTU

SOUTH AFRICA

WHAT IS UBUNTU?

'I am, because of you.' This is the essence of ubuntu, an African humanist philosophy of oneness, connectedness and humanity. Ubuntu is not specific to South Africa or only the southern African region; over the years the philosophy has become widespread across the entire continent (*see* p.144). At the core of ubuntu is human kindness and the importance of community, open-heartedness and mutual caring. It's about recognising how we cannot exist in isolation as individuals, we are all part of something bigger and that is what being a human is all about. We all have a vital role to play in the world and it's not just about ourselves but what we can do to make it a better place for everyone around us, too.

In the 1990s, ubuntu started to become more well known around the globe when it became the core of the anti-apartheid movement and was used as a political philosophy in writings and speeches by Nelson Mandela and Archbishop Desmond Tutu. Ubuntu does not discount that people and political parties will not have their differences, but it recognises these differences and sees them as a building block for reconciliation.

Nobel Peace Prize winner and a leader of the anti-apartheid movement, Archbishop Desmond Tutu introduced the West to ubuntu. When he was asked to be the chairman of South Africa's Truth and Reconciliation Commission, the archbishop drew on the concept of ubuntu. Through coming together as one, South Africa was able to reckon with its history of apartheid and move away from being such a divided country.

More than ever, ubuntu is vital for sustaining humanity and the planet, we need to move towards a less individualistic view and come back to more of a community spirit in our everyday lives. It requires a monumental shift in how we all view one another, all living things and the planet itself.

Nelson Mandela's incredible life's work in the fight against oppression was heavily inspired by ubuntu – he was the epitome of the ideology, a man prepared to give up his life to see equality, justice and freedom for his country. Mandela passed away in 2013 and in former US President Barack Obama's tribute he said: 'Mandela understood the ties that bind the human spirit. There is a word in South Africa – Ubuntu – that describes his greatest gift: his recognition that we are all bound together in ways that can be invisible to the eye; that there is a oneness to humanity; that we achieve ourselves by sharing ourselves with others, and caring for those around us.'

Ubuntu can be a very powerful concept and one that has the ability to benefit the entire world. It's clear that important change can happen if we all start to live a little more by the ubuntu philosophy.

WHERE DOES UBUNTU ORIGINATE?

Some historians suggest that the word ubuntu has appeared in writing since at least 1846. The origin of the word and its concept can be traced back to the Nguni peoples, Bantu-speaking ethnic groups living in southern Africa, mainly Zimbabwe, South Africa and eSwatini (formerly Swaziland). It is said to come from a set of closely related Nguni languages, mainly the Zulu and Xhosa languages. In the Shona language, spoken in Zimbabwe, ubuntu is unhu, and in Uganda and Tanzania it is known as obuntu. Though the word is slightly different, the concept is much the same.

There is a Nguni proverb 'umuntu ngumuntu ngabantu' that can be translated loosely as 'a person is a person through other persons.' Ubuntu is often described in relation to this proverb.

WHAT ARE THE HEALTH AND HAPPINESS BENEFITS?

Ubuntu is at the core of humanity and how we act towards each other, so the benefits of a society following it as a philosophy are fairly obvious. If we take an individualistic view, every person for themselves, then we are missing the point of what it means to be human. Without ubuntu we are acting selfishly, greedily and with disrespect for others in our society. Though if we practice ubuntu, we are truly connecting with others, living with dignity, harmony, understanding and community. Everyone wants to feel appreciated, cared for, important and respected. Ubuntu helps us all achieve this.

The effects of ubuntu can be far-reaching. Start with your family, your neighbours, your community, it can then take on a ripple effect that reaches across the globe. It's the act of paying it forward, one act of kindness inspires another and so on. Though ubuntu is not an individualistic pursuit, by letting ubuntu guide our actions it leads us to becoming kinder and more thoughtful as individuals. Ubuntu means we are all interconnected, no one lives in isolation and no one is left behind. There is no place for judgement, discrimination or hatred with ubuntu. People work together towards common goals – everyone helps everyone.

Ubuntu doesn't just have significant social advantages, it can also be applied to our working environments. Living by the philosophies of ubuntu can help create happier and more harmonious workplaces, it can empower people and create better leaders. When we act with more compassion and empathy, support each other and realise we are all in it together, it can lead to a more efficient and effective organisation.

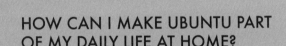

HOW CAN I MAKE UBUNTU PART OF MY DAILY LIFE AT HOME?

We can all demonstrate ubuntu through our actions and the way we interact with those around us. Ask yourself these questions: 'Are my actions benefiting not just me but the people around me?' and 'What is important to me, what are my values and how do they align with the greater community and the global world?'

These are huge questions and points to think about and you might not have the answers straight away, but it's a great jumping-off point to start self-reflection and move towards a more holistic way of living and interacting.

If you are thinking about trying to become a person with more ubuntu in their daily life, ask yourself what would that look like? What would the change be for you? What simple acts of kindness could you make in your life?

Expressing ubuntu doesn't need to be a mammoth undertaking, you don't need to completely change who you are or quit your job to start volunteering. It can be done with simple acts, such as helping a neighbour with their shopping or offering someone a lift to work or just listening and showing care and understanding when a friend tells you about a problem they're having. Or it might be something larger like volunteering at your local community centre or for a not-for-profit organisation. When you give back to your community, it also gives back to you.

When you think about ubuntu and how to start living by it, it helps to keep in mind the traits that someone with ubuntu might have.

Empathy   Compassion

Generosity   Vulnerability

Open-mindedness   Kindness

Looking after one another in a society plays a pivotal role in the success of humanity. Let's all try and learn from Africa's philosophy of ubuntu as we move towards the future.

YOGA

INDIA

WHAT IS YOGA?

We are familiar with yoga – having been lured in by the long list of health and wellbeing benefits – and have been working on perfecting our downward dog for a while now. Yoga has become a huge global trend in the health and wellness world and there are many different ideas and styles, but what actually is at its core?

Rooted in ancient Indian philosophy, yoga is a practice for the mind and body through the combination of physical postures and movement (known as asanas), breathing techniques (pranayama) and meditation (dyana); in essence, it's a system of self-realisation. In more recent times, the wellness world has run with it, altered it, moulded it in various ways, and commercialised it, and it can now mean different things to different people.

Classical yoga or hatha yoga is known by most people, but there are loads of yoga styles out there. Some of the more popular and well-known styles are described on page 150.

HATHA

Hatha yoga refers to any physical based yoga that uses sequences of asanas (postures or poses) and is differentiated from the traditional non-movement spiritual yoga practices. It's a gentler, slower style of yoga that is good for beginners as it incorporates basic asana, meditation and breathing exercises.

ASHTANGA

Ashtanga is a more dynamic style of yoga designed to build up a bit more heat in the body. It's a highly structured style featuring a specific sequence of poses that need to be mastered before moving onto the next; these become more strenuous as students advance. Ashtanga is based on traditional practices and was popularised in the West by Indian yoga teacher, K. Pattabhi Jois who established the Ashtanga Yoga Research Institute in Mysuru (Mysore), India in 1948.

VINYASA

This one is for those looking for a real workout and to be physically challenged. Vinyasa yoga is a fast-paced style where students coordinate their breath with movement to flow from one pose to the next.

IYENGAR

Iyengar is a meticulous and highly disciplined style of yoga that was developed in the 1960s by the late Indian guru, B.K.S Iyengar. The emphasis is on alignment and precision with postures and breathing exercises and the use of props to facilitate, such as blocks, bolsters and yoga ropes.

BIKRAM

Some like it hot, and some favour Bikram yoga! This sweaty and, let's get real, stinky style involves a series of poses in a hot room, usually somewhere between 35–42°C/95–107°F. It is popular for those who enjoy a physically demanding and challenging style.

WHERE DOES YOGA ORIGINATE?

Yoga is an ancient Indian philosophy and spiritual practice that may date back as far as 5000 years. It's thought that the word 'yoga' comes from the Sanskrit word 'yuj', which means yoke, bind or union, and this is often interpreted as the union between mind, body and breath, though its etymology is debated.

Patanjali is often referred to by many as the 'father of ashtanga yoga', thanks to his classic text *Yoga Sutra*, widely considered the authoritative writing on yoga. The text provides a framework for the practice of yoga and outlines the eight limbs associated with ashtanga yoga, which act as guidelines for the philosophy and how to live a more meaningful life:

1. Yamas: Restraints, moral and ethical codes of conduct, including truthfulness and non-violence.
2. Niyamas: Spiritual observances or positive duties – going to temple or church, saying grace, meditating.
3. Asana: Postures.
4. Pranayama: Breathing techniques.
5. Pratyahara: Sensory withdrawal – drawing inward and away from external stimuli.
6. Dharana: Concentration.
7. Dhyana: Meditation.
8. Samadhi: Bliss, enlightenment – the final step of the journey in self-realisation.

Yoga is a huge industry with proven heath and wellness benefits, but the origins of it can sometimes be lost when there are boutiques charging hefty prices for classes and designer 'yoga wear' and luxury yoga mats touted as essential accessories. Don't forget this is a spiritual philosophy that is strongly rooted in ancient Indian tradition. Yoga is about coming back to the self and living a pure life, and when you participate in the practice you'll be fortunate enough to reap some of those health and wellbeing benefits along the way, too.

WHAT ARE THE HEALTH AND HAPPINESS BENEFITS?

There have been countless studies on the positive physical and mental effects of yoga and the list of reported health and wellbeing benefits is long and broad.

Increases flexibility, muscle strength and tone

Helps weight loss

Improves cardiovascular health

Increases blood flow

Boosts immunity

Decreases blood pressure

Improves mood and helps fight off depression and anxiety

Relaxes you and helps you to focus

Maintains nervous system

Improves sleep

Helps with gastrointestinal issues

Lowers stress levels

May reduce inflammation

May help with reducing chronic pain

Relieves period pain

The breathing and meditation techniques work to calm the body down and, in turn, send a message to the brain to calm also. It can work to reduce and control the body's flight or fight response (the sympathetic nervous system), as well as the parasympathetic nervous system, which lets you know to calm down.

The Boston University School of Medicine conducted a study in 2019, which was published online in the *Journal of Psychiatric Practice*, and provided evidence that yoga can improve symptoms of anxiety and depression. And the more you do it, the more improvement is made longer term.

So whether you are looking to lose weight, improve your focus and concentration at work, deal with anxiety or depression, get help with chronic pain or you're just looking for a better night's sleep, jumping on a yoga mat may well be the answer.

WHERE IN INDIA CAN I EXPERIENCE YOGA?

The best place to try yoga is, of course, its homeland – India. You'll find hundreds of schools and ashrams dotted all over the country with classes to suit everyone from greener-than-green beginners to master yogis.

Two of the main epicentres for yoga are Rishikesh in the north, the birthplace of yoga and known as the Yoga Capital of the World, and Mysuru (Mysore) in the south, which is where ashtanga originated.

Be sure to do your research before signing up to any school or ashram, as teaching standards and styles vary widely. Check out the school's reputation and the teachers' qualifications. Where did they train and how much experience do they have? What style of classes do they have – beginner, advanced, something that will suit your level? What is the philosophy of their practice and does this ring true – does it seem genuine?

Recommended yoga schools and ashram include:

- IndeaYoga, Mysuru (Mysore): Run by guru Bharath Shetty (*see* p.156), who practiced under the late B.K.S. Iyengar. See: indeayoga.com
- Abhayaranya Rishikesh Yogpeeth Yoga Village, Rishikesh. See: abhayaranya.business.site
- Anand Prakash Yoga Ashram, Rishikesh. See: akhandayoga.com/ashram
- Shri K Pattabhi Jois Ashtanga Yoga Shala, Mysuru (Mysore): Founded by the renowned teacher K. Pattabhi Jois. See: kpjayshala.com

You can also try timing your visit for the first week of March when thousands of yoga masters from around the globe head to Rishikesh for the International Yoga Festival. See: internationalyogafestival.org.

HOW CAN I MAKE YOGA PART OF MY DAILY LIFE AT HOME?

The great thing about yoga is that you don't need much to get started. There are plenty of courses and classes and you are bound to find one local to you. You can also find numerous online classes where you can do yoga in the comfort of your home – though it might be a good idea to do a few teacher-guided classes first to understand the basics and the correct postures to ensure you don't injure yourself. Then grab yourself a yoga mat and maybe a towel or blanket, and a spare space in your home, and get stretching.

You can find classes to suit whatever your skill level or time constraints might be. If you can only spare 30 minutes here and there, that's fine. But if you have the time, aim for a few one-hour sessions a week to truly get the most out of it and to experience all the health and wellbeing benefits.

There is no right or wrong style of yoga – it's about finding what suits you and what your personal preference is. Ask yourself: What style appeals to me more – gentle and slow, or fast-paced and dynamic? Am I looking for something physically demanding or something more restorative? Will I most likely do yoga in the morning to help me feel invigorated and start the day or to wind down at night to help with sleeping? Am I hoping to tap into the traditional and spiritual side of yoga, or do I prefer the more modern style? Then hop online and do some research to find classes that match what you're after.

INTERVIEW
Bharath Shetty

Yoga instructor at IndeaYoga, Mysuru (Mysore), India.

WHEN DID YOU FIRST START PRACTICING YOGA AND WHY WERE YOU INTERESTED IN IT?

I first started in June of 1993 to overcome asthma. When I was listening to a lecture about yoga, the professor was explaining what yoga is good for and one of the things he said was asthma – and that resonated with me. Over the next few years I did self-practice and I never went back. After two years my asthma drastically reduced and I had almost no symptoms until 2007. I had symptoms then because I was under a lot of pressure while building my shala in Gokulam. I had two young daughters, I was very stressed, and I was missing my practice. This was a reminder for me to not stress about life.

HOW HAS YOGA IMPACTED YOUR LIFE?

First of all, there was a huge change in my asthma after the first two years. Then yoga reduced my short-tempered mind. I was spending a lot of time alone before. In 1999 I met with an accident where a bus passed over both of my legs. Yoga helped me recover very quickly, even though the doctors told me I would never walk again. It taught me that 'impossible' is nothing. I had a hernia in the year 2000, following my accident, and yoga helped me to recover from that without surgery. With my students, I can see so many people recover from their health issues. Between 1995 and 2000 I was able to see that yoga helped people to overcome their health issues and it kept them happier. That's how IndeaYoga's vision came to be: health and bliss for all. This has kept me going until now, happy and healthy. It has also motivated me to train yoga teachers. I want to reach the entire world, and that's why I started teaching teachers.

WHAT STYLE OF YOGA DO YOU TEACH AND WHAT DREW YOU TO THAT PARTICULAR STYLE?

I teach IndeaYoga. It is based on the Iyengar based hatha (without props) and Krishnamacharya's ashtanga system. There are three different areas we work on: aarogya (health), abhyasa (practice), and ananda (bliss). Mainly we concentrate on the coordination between body, breath and mind. The meaning of IndeaYoga is: 'In' for inner and 'dea' meaning light. It's all about finding our own inner bliss. Mainly my practice is based on Iyengar's *Light on Yoga* and that led to IndeaYoga. This is more dynamic and alignment based. Additionally I added breath coordination, which helps to withdraw the sense organs. I emphasise balance between right and left to keep a good balance of the sympathetic and parasympathetic nervous systems (Ida and Pingala).

WHAT DO YOU HOPE YOUR STUDENTS GET FROM ONE OF YOUR YOGA CLASSES AND HOW DO YOU WANT THEM TO FEEL?

After the class one should feel that nothing can distract them. They're just floating. Any noise, any distraction, any shouting, there is no reaction to it. One should experience the sense withdrawal (pratyahara). They should feel the great balance between the body and the breath, which leads the mind to stay calm throughout the day. In one hour one should experience the freshness of every day. Our classes are all about bringing balance between body, breath and mind and experiencing the samyama (the combination of Dharana, Dhyana, and Samadhi, or simply the different stages of meditation).

ZEN MEDITATION

JAPAN

WHAT IS ZEN MEDITATION?

Meditation may have been mostly affiliated with monks in the past but this mindfulness practice is becoming a popular and valuable tool for many people facing increasing stress and anxiety. Meditation is undertaken to encourage a heightened state of awareness and attention to achieve a clearer mind and more stable emotions.

Zen meditation is an ancient Buddhist practice, which usually involves being seated and paying attention to the breath and clearing the mind by observing things, but just letting go of thoughts and feelings that arise – without fixating on them. Zazen (seated meditation) is at the heart of Buddhist Zen meditation – za meaning sitting, and zen meaning meditation in Japanese. Zen meditation doesn't just aim to create a sense of calm and relaxation, it also aims to delve a little deeper into a spiritual awakening.

A classic feature of Zen meditation in Japan is the Zen garden. Buddhist monks in Japan created Zen gardens as a place to meditate and help calm the mind. Known as kare-sansui, meaning dry-landscape gardens, these are usually made up of raked gravel, sand, stones, moss and pruned trees, but never include a water element – as the name suggests. The sand and gravel is meticulously raked into patterns to represent rippling water, while the rocks typically symbolise mountains. These gardens provide a tranquil spot to promote reflection and Zen meditation.

WHERE DOES ZEN MEDITATION ORIGINATE?

Buddhism originated in India over 2500 years ago and was founded by Siddhartha Gautama (the Buddha). It arrived in Japan sometime in the 6th century CE, via China and Korea along the ancient trade route network – the Silk Road.

Several different sects of Japanese Buddhism developed in Japan over the centuries, though Zen is perhaps the most well-known. There are two main schools of Zen in Japan – Soto and Rinzai Zen. The Soto school has seated meditation at its core, while the Rinzai school is known for using koans – these are a type of spiritual riddle that a Zen master presents to a student. Some good examples of koans are the riddles: 'What is the sound of one hand clapping?' and 'If a tree falls in the woods and there is no one around to hear it, does it still make a sound?' It's hoped that by attempting to answer a koan, a student will overcome rational thought and be triggered into transcendental thinking.

WHAT ARE THE HEALTH AND HAPPINESS BENEFITS?

Meditation in general offers a bounty of reported health and wellbeing benefits. Zen Buddhism is a religion that offers a path to enlightenment through meditation, but even if you don't quite manage to achieve enlightenment, there are plenty of other great reasons for practicing it – from spiritual to physical and mental health benefits.

Studies show that practicing Zen meditation can provide the necessary tools for coping with anxiety, stress and depression. It provides an insight into the workings of the mind and a way of slowing down and experiencing calm and peace of mind.

Other benefits include:

Better sleep

Improved immune system

Reduced sensitivity to pain

Improved posture by helping to strengthen the back muscles

Improved blood flow

Reduced blood pressure

WHERE IN JAPAN CAN I EXPERIENCE ZEN MEDITATION?

Almost all of the Zen temple grounds in Japan feature kare-sansui gardens and these are the perfect places to explore unguided and to find a quiet spot for meditation. Some of the country's most famous Zen gardens are found in Kyoto.

KYOTO'S ZEN GARDENS

Ryōan-ji is an absolute favourite of mine for its sublime collection of rocks sitting on a vast 'sea' of sand. Its popularity means it can get overrun with visitors, so it's best to try to visit early in the morning on a weekday.

Daitoku-ji is a Zen temple complex in the north-west of the city and is the perfect place to spend hours strolling along its cobbled laneways and ducking in and out of the atmospheric temples to sit quietly in awe of its exquisite kare-sansui gardens.

The oldest Zen temple in Kyoto is Kennin-ji and it's located close to the bustling Gion district. I have a particular fondness for the Zen garden here, as it provides a welcome respite from the hordes of tourists and the crowds that take over the Gion area.

OKU-NO-IN TEMPLE, KŌYA-SAN

The mountaintop temple complex Kōya-san is one of the most spiritual places in Japan and the centre of Shingon Buddhism. This sect of Buddhism was introduced to Japan by one of the country's most significant religious figures, Kōbō Daishi. At the far end of Kōya-san is the Gobyō, the crypt that Kōbō Daishi entered to begin his eternal meditation. The Oku-no-in temple (meaning 'inner sanctuary') is the site of Daishi's mausoleum. Some of the temples at Koya-san offer guests the chance to stay overnight and dine on traditional Buddhist vegetarian cuisine and to wake up for morning meditation with the monks, otherwise it's an easy daytrip from Osaka.

SHUNKŌ-IN, KYOTO

A sub-temple of Kyoto's Myoshin-ji temple, Shunkō-in is run by the American-educated fifth-generation Buddhist priest Takafumi Kawakami (*see* p.166). The Zen meditation classes are held in English and are followed by a tour of the temple. In these classes students learn the basics of Zen meditation and how to incorporate the Zen philosophy into their everyday life.
See: shunkoin.com

HOW CAN I MAKE ZEN MEDITATION PART OF MY DAILY LIFE AT HOME?

Don't worry if your garden is more chaos than Zen or you live in an apartment sans garden. It's fairly easy to incorporate Zen meditation into your daily life regardless of where you live and how busy your schedule might be. And while a trip to Japan or a perfectly manicured Zen garden at home might be a lovely idea, thankfully it's not an essential requirement. All you really need to start practicing a bit of zazen (seated meditation) is a bum to sit on (tick) and some household items, such as a comfortable cushion, thick blanket or a chair.

Before starting your session, find a quiet, peaceful spot where you hopefully won't be disturbed by children, pets, partners or noise. You want to try to create as serene an atmosphere as you can. Ideally that room or place will have some light, not too bright or too dark, and be at a comfortable temperature so you won't get too hot or freezing cold halfway through – chattering teeth or sweat running down the brow make it tough to focus!

Traditionally, zazen is practiced by sitting in the half lotus (with one foot on top of the opposite thigh, and the other foot on the floor underneath the other thigh) or full lotus position (each foot on the opposite thigh with the line of the toes matching the outer line of the thighs) on a zafu (a thick, round cushion). However, if you're not flexible, you might feel more comfortable kneeling or sitting on a chair. Choose where you will feel most comfortable to be able to hold a position for a period of time. If that's not in the lotus position, don't worry. If you're seated on a chair, be sure to try not to lean on the backrest, instead focus on your posture being upright to the sky.

Once you've gotten yourself comfortable, pick a spot around a metre in front of you to direct your vision, without really focusing on anything in particular. Try to rest your eyes in a half open, half closed position. Next, try to establish a calm, deep, natural breathing rhythm – this is a fundamental part of Zen meditation. Breathe quietly through your nose and keep your mouth closed. The inhalation will occur naturally, so you just want to focus on your exhalation.

It's normal to have thoughts and feelings arise when you are practicing Zen meditation. It's not about trying to block these out but instead letting them float by you without pursuing them or paying them any attention. Think of these thoughts as clouds rolling by past you. The more you meditate, the easier this will become.

Try starting out with five-minute sessions as a beginner, and then increase the amount of time by a few minutes each session as you gain more experience and comfort with the activity. In a matter of weeks you should be able to work up to 30-minute sessions or longer – whatever feels comfortable for you.

INTERVIEW
Rev. Takafumi Kawakami

From the Shunkō-in temple, Kyoto, Japan.

WHEN DID YOU FIRST START PRACTICING ZEN BUDDHISM AND HOW DID YOUR LIFE LEAD YOU TO IT?

My first practice of meditation started when I was in high school. But I didn't call it Zen meditation. I was just focusing my breath to improve my focus during my weightlifting practice. My interest in Zen Buddhism and its practice started growing when I was in a college in the USA, I studied Buddhism and other religious study classes as the requirements for my psychology major. Even though I was born in my family temple, Shunkō-in temple in Kyoto and grew up there as the fifth-generation Buddhist priest, I had never studied Buddhism academically. The intellectual understanding of Buddhism led me to be brought back to my family tradition.

WHAT DO YOU CONSIDER TO BE THE THREE MOST IMPORTANT THINGS IN THE PROCESS OF ZEN MEDITATION?

Firstly, it is not about emptying your mind and feeling calm. The meditation is observation of your reactions to what is happening inside and outside of you (intuition, impression,

feelings, emotions and sensations). Secondly, try to find out what kind of beliefs are behind your reactions. Thirdly, contemplate how you formed your beliefs and see how your reactions can be changed if you modify or remove them.

WHAT ADVICE CAN YOU GIVE TO SOMEONE WHO HAS NEVER PRACTISED MEDITATION BEFORE AND WOULD LIKE TO START?

Try to meditate at the same place and at the same time. Also, I recommend people to create a routine, like waking up, drinking a glass of water, and then meditation.

THERE ARE MANY REPORTED HEALTH AND WELLBEING BENEFITS OF MEDITATION, WHAT ARE YOUR THOUGHTS ON THESE?

I acknowledge various researchers on meditation and wellbeing. In fact, I've worked on some wellbeing projects with public health researchers and cognitive scientists. Public enthusiasm for meditation sometimes ignores the actual scientific understanding of the effects of meditation on our wellbeing. Thus, just doing the meditation doesn't make you happy. You have to learn the philosophies behind Zen and other Buddhist or Eastern contemplation practices.

HOW CAN PEOPLE BENEFIT BY INCORPORATING ZEN MEDITATION PRINCIPLES INTO THEIR DAILY LIVES?

Meditation without philosophy is just another stress-reduction technique. But if you practice meditation with philosophy you can learn about the humility and curiosity in your life. Also, you stop running away from the uncertainty or difficulty in your life. You start to lean in to them.

FURTHER READING

Print

Berlin, Isaiah, *The Roots of Romanticism*, Vintage, 2000

Brones, Anna & Kindvall, Johanna, *Fika : The Art of the Swedish Coffee Break*, Penguin Random House, 2015

Brones, Anna, *Live lagom : Balanced Living, the Swedish Way*, Ebury Press, 2017

Curran, Stuart, *The Cambridge Companion to British Romanticism*, 2nd ed, Cambridge, 2010

De Surany, Caroline, *The Book of Ikigai*, Hardie Grant, 2018

García, Héctor & Miralles, Francesc , *Ikigai: The Japanese Secret to a Long and Happy Life*, Cornerstone, 2017

García, Héctor & Miralles, Francesc, *Forest Bathing: The Rejuvenating Practice of Shinrin Yoku*, Tuttle Publishing, 2020

Goldberg, Michelle, *The Goddess Pose : the Audacious Life of Indra Devi, the Woman who Helped Bring Yoga to the West*, New York: Alfred A Knopf, 2015

Li, Dr Qing, *Forest Bathing: How Trees Can Help You Find Health and Happiness*, Penguin Life, 2018

Masuno, Shunmyō, *Zen: The Art of Simple Living*, Penguin, 2019

Mogi, Ken, *The Little Book of Ikigai*, Quercus an imprint of Hachette, 2017

Nylund, Joanna, *Sisu: The Finnish Art of Courage*, Octopus Publishing, 2018

Pantzar, Katja, *Finding Sisu: In Search of Courage, Strength and Happiness the Finnish Way*, Hodder & Stoughton, 2018

Soderberg, Marie Tourell, *Hygge: The Danish Art of Happiness*, Penguin, 2016

Tutu, Desmond, *No Future Without Forgiveness*, Penguin, 2000

Wiking, Meik, *The Little Book of Hygge*, Penguin, 2016

Online

www.grossnationalhappiness.com

www.happinessresearchinstitute.com

ww.slowfood.com

www.taichiforhealthinstitute.org

www.ted.com

https://worldhappiness.report

INDEX

Abbhayaranya Rishikesh Yogpeeth
  Yoga Village, Rishikesh 154
Addis Ababa, Ethiopia 13
agate 21
Akasawa Natural Recreational Forest,
  Kiso, Nagano, Japan 111
aloha spirit x-7
Aloha Spirit Law x-7
Amalfi Coast, Italy 28
amethyst 21
Amsterdam, The Netherlands 53
Anand Prakash Yoga Ashram,
  Rishikesh 154
Anogia, Crete 84
art
  Heraklion Archaeological
    Museum, Crete 85
  Japan 76
  National Archaeological Museum,
    Athens, Greece 85
  National Gallery, Athens,
    Greece 85
Ashtanga yoga 150
Athens, Greece 84-5
Athens & Epidaurus festival,
  Greece 84

bakeries & treats, Copenhagen,
  Denmark 70
Baudelaire, Charles 98
Beethoven, Ludwig van 99
Beijing, China 137
Bhutan, Gross National Happiness
  (GNH) 56-63
Bikram yoga 150
Blake, William 98, 102
bloodstone 22

Brones, Anna 40-1
Brothers Grimm 100
Bund, The, Shanghai, China 137
Byron, Lord 98

Cafe Hoppe, Amsterdam,
  The Netherlands 53
calcite 21
carnelian 22
Chen style, tai chi, China 134
China, tai chi 132-9
Chuan-yu, Wu 127
Chubu-Sangaku National Park,
  Japan 111
cinnamon buns (recipe) 39
Cockermouth, Cumbria, England 102
coffee ceremony 8-15
Coffee Collective, Copenhagen,
  Denmark 70
Coleridge Cottage, Nether Stowey,
  Somerset, England 103
Coleridge, Samuel Taylor 98, 103
Constable, John viii, 98, 101-2
cooking classes, Japan 76
Copenhagen, Denmark 69
Costa Rica, pura vida 88-95
crystal and stone healing 16-23

dance, Greece 84
De Sluyswacht, Amsterdam,
  The Netherlands 53
Delacroix, Eugène 98
Denmark, hygge 64-71
dog-sledding, Norway 47
dolce far niente 24-31
Dora Stratou Dance Theatre,
  Athens, Greece 84

England, Romanticism 96–105
Ethiopia, coffee ceremony 8–15
fika 32–41
Finland, sisu 116–23
forest bathing, Japan 106–15
friluftsliv 42–9

Galani Cafe, Ethiopia 13
Gallup 4, 91, 118
Gautama, Siddhartha (the
   Buddha) 160
gezelligheid 50–5
Goya, Francois 98
Grasmere, Cumbria, England 102
Greece, meraki 80–7
Greek National Opera, Greece 85
Gros, Antoine-Jean 98
Gross National Happiness (GNH) 56–63

Hasegawa, Akihiro 75
Hatha yoga 150
Hawaii, aloha spirit x–7
Heraklion Archaeological Museum,
   Crete 85
hiking, Japan 76, 111
hygge 64–71

ikigai 72–9
IndeaYoga, Mysuru (Mysore) 154
India, yoga 148–57
In't Aepjen, Amsterdam,
   The Netherlands 53
Italy
   dolce far niente 24–31
   Slow Food 124–31
Iyengar yoga 150

jade 22
Jægersborggade, Copenhagen,
   Denmark 69

Japan
   ikigai 72–9
   shinrin yoku 106–15
   zen meditation 158–67
Jotunheimen National Park, Norway 46

Kafa Coffee Museum, Ethiopia 13
Kamiya, Mieko 79
kanelbullar (recipe) 39
Kawakami, Rev. Takafumi 166–7
Keats, John 98, 103
Koso, Nagano, Japan 111
Kōya-san, Japan 162
Kyoto, Japan 162, 163

Li, Dr Qing 114–15
Lillehammer region, Norway 47
Liszt, Frank 99
London, England 103

Mandela, Nelson 140, 143
maraki 80–7
Megaron, The, Athens, Greece 84
Mogi, Ken 79
Mount Takao, Japan 111
music
   Anogia, Crete 84
   Japan 77
   The Megaron, Athens, Greece 84

National Archaeological Museum,
   Athens, Greece 85
National Gallery, Athens, Greece 85
Nether Stowey, Somerset, England 103
Netherlands, The, gezelligheid 50–5
Norway, friluftsliv 42–9

Obama, Barack 143
Oku-no-in Temple, Kōya-san, Japan 162
opera, Greek National Opera, Greece 85

Pantzar, Katja 122-3
Patanjali 135
Petrini, Carlo 127
Piedmont, Italy 129
Poe, Edgar Allen 99
Positano, Italy 129
Preikestolen (Pulpit Rock), Norway 46
pura vida 88-95

quartz 22

Romanticism 96-105
Rome's piazzas, Italy 28

Sardinia, Italy 129
Shanghai, China 137
Shelley, Percy Bysshe 98
Shetty, Bharath 156-7
shinrin yoku 106-15
Shri K Pattabhi Jois Ashtanga Yoga
    Shala, Mysuru (Mysore) 154
Shunkō-in, Kyoto, Japan 163
sisu 116-23
Shelley, Mary 98
skiing, Lillehammer region,
    Norway 47
Slow Food 124-31
snowmobiling, Svalbard, Norway 47
Somerset, England 103
South Africa, ubuntu 140-7
sports, Japan 77
Sun style, tai chi, China 134
Svalbard, Norway 47
Sweden, fika 32-41

tai chi 132-9
Tate Britain, London, England 103
Tchaikovsky, Pyotr Ilyich 99
Temple of Heaven, Beijing, China 137
The Bund, Shanghai, China 137

The Megaron, Athens, Greece 84
The Netherlands, gezelligheid 50-5
Tivoli Gardens, Copenhagen,
    Denmark 69
Tomaco, Addis Ababa, Ethiopia 13
Tomoca, Ethopia 13
Turner, J.M.W. viii, 98, 101-4
Tuscany, Italy 29, 129
Tutu, Desmond 140, 142, 146

ubuntu 140-7
UN 59
USA, aloha spirit x-7
USA, crystal and stone healing 16-23

Venice, Italy 29
Villa Carlotta, Lake Como, Italy 28
Vinyasa yoga 150

Wagner, Richard 99
Whitman, Walt 99
Winchester, England 103
Wordsworth House & Garden,
    Cockermouth, Cumbria,
    England 102
Wordsworth, William 98, 102
World Bank 61
World Happiness Report 35, 42, 61,
    66, 88, 91, 118,
Wu style, tai chi, China 134
Wudang Shan, Hubei province,
    China 137

Yakushima National Park, Japan 111
Yang style, tai chi, China 134
yoga 148-57

Zen gardens, Kyoto, Japan 162
zen meditation 158-67
Zhang 135

ABOUT THE AUTHOR

Kate Morgan is a freelance travel writer and editor from Melbourne, Australia. Through her travels over the years she has learned first-hand the many ways people around the world strive for happiness and wellbeing. She has spent time meditating in Buddhist temples in Kyoto, Japan; appreciated the art of gezelligheid when researching Amsterdam in the Netherlands; indulged in traditional cooking in the Slow Food birth town of Piedmont, Italy; and practiced Ashtanga yoga in Mysuru (Mysore), India. Kate has worked in-house at Lonely Planet as a commissioning editor, and also written for various travel guidebooks, online and on magazines for companies such as Lonely Planet, BBC Travel, Condé Nast Traveller, Broadsheet Media, Waitrose Magazine in the UK, Visit Victoria and Tourism Australia. Kate was also a contributor to Lonely Planet's *Wellness Escapes* guide.

Published in 2020 by Hardie Grant Travel,
a division of Hardie Grant Publishing

Hardie Grant Travel (Melbourne)
Building 1, 658 Church Street
Richmond, Victoria 3121

Hardie Grant Travel (Sydney)
Level 7, 45 Jones Street
Ultimo, NSW 2007

www.hardiegrant.com/au/travel

The Globetrotter's Guide to Happiness
ISBN 9781741177091

10 9 8 7 6 5 4 3 2 1

Publisher Melissa Kayser
Project editor Megan Cuthbert
Editor Alice Barker
Proofreader Judith Bamber
Design Andy Warren
Typesetting Hannah Schubert
Index Max McMaster

Colour reproduction by Hannah Schubert
and Splitting Image Colour Studio

Printed and bound in China by
LEO Paper Products LTD.

A catalogue record for this
book is available from the
National Library of Australia

FSC
www.fsc.org
MIX
Paper from
responsible sources
FSC® C020056

Hardie Grant acknowledges the Traditional
Owners of the country on which we work,
the Wurundjeri people of the Kulin nation
and the Gadigal people of the Eora nation, and
recognises their continuing connection to the
land, waters and culture. We pay our respects
to their Elders past, present and emerging.

The paper this book is printed on is from
FSC®-certified forests and other sources.
FSC® promotes environmentally responsible,
socially beneficial and economically viable
management of the world's forests.